Crisis in the Kindergarten

Why Children Need to Play in School

Edward Miller and Joan Almon

Alliance for Childhood

First printing March 2009
ISBN: 978-0-9823751-0-5
Printed in the United States of America

Alliance for Childhood
P.O. Box 444
College Park, MD 20741
Tel/Fax 301-779-1033

Crisis in the Kindergarten is also available online at
www.allianceforchildhood.org.

Suggested citation for this book:
Edward Miller and Joan Almon, *Crisis in the
Kindergarten: Why Children Need to Play in School*,
College Park, MD: Alliance for Childhood, 2009.

Graphic design by Sonya Cohen Cramer, Takoma Park, Maryland

THE ALLIANCE FOR CHILDHOOD is a nonprofit partnership of educators, health professionals, and other advocates for children who are concerned about the decline in children's health and well-being and who share a sense that childhood itself is endangered. The Alliance was founded in 1999 and is incorporated in the state of Maryland. It is funded entirely by grants and donations from individuals, foundations, and businesses.

The Alliance promotes policies and practices that support children's healthy development, love of learning, and joy in living. Our public education campaigns bring to light both the promise and the vulnerability of childhood. We act for the sake of the children themselves and for a more just, democratic, and ecologically responsible future.

The Alliance's current work focuses on the recovery of creative play, which is disappearing from childhood, and on the need for a more ethics-based and mindful approach to teaching technology literacy. For information on how you can support the Alliance's work, visit our web site: **www.allianceforchildhood.org**.

CONTENTS

ACKNOWLEDGMENTS

WE ARE DEEPLY GRATEFUL to the many people who contributed to this report. The Alliance for Childhood received funding for the three research studies and the report itself from the Woodshouse Foundation, the Buffett Early Childhood Fund, the NoVo Foundation, RSF Social Finance, the Kalliopeia Foundation, Bay Area Early Childhood Funders, the Newman's Own Foundation, and Community Playthings. Their commitment to the education and well-being of young children is greatly appreciated.

The three research teams worked very hard to develop new tools for research and to share their results with us in concise, clear ways. They include Jennifer Astuto at Long Island University and LaRue Allen at New York University; Jan Drucker, Margery Franklin, and Barbara Schecter at Sarah Lawrence College; and Allison Fuligni and Sandra Hong at the University of California, Los Angeles. Their findings were supplemented by interviews with Nancy Carlsson-Paige and Diane Levin.

Preliminary results of the studies were discussed at a meeting in May 2008 at Sarah Lawrence College, and the feedback of participants was important to the framing and writing of the report. The participants included members of the Alliance for Childhood Board of Trustees: Marilyn Benoit, Bill Crain, Elizabeth Goodenough, and Lowell Monke. Some members of the National Advisory Board listed below were in attendance as were others who provided expertise in child development, health, and related fields: Wendy Blackwell, Cheryl French, Rachel Grob, Susan Ohanian, and Mark Schlesinger.

Particular thanks go to the members of the Alliance's National Advisory Board. Many of them read draft chapters and gave us advice and assistance as the report was being written. We appreciate their help but take full responsibility for any errors in the final version.

Preface

T HE ARGUMENT OF THIS REPORT, that child-initiated play must be restored to kindergarten, will be dismissed and even ridiculed in some quarters. In spite of the fact that the vital importance of play in young children's development has been shown in study after study, many people believe that play is a waste of time in school. School, they say, should be a place for learning. There's plenty of time for play at home.

Skepticism about the value of play is compounded by the widespread assumption—promoted by hundreds of "smart baby" products—that the earlier children begin to master the basic elements of reading, such as phonics and letter recognition, the more likely they are to succeed in school. And so kindergarten education has become heavily focused on teaching literacy and other academic skills, and preschool is rapidly following suit.

The common misconceptions about young children's play fall apart when we look closely at what is really going on. We begin to be able to differentiate between superficial play and the complex make-believe play that can engage five-year-olds for an hour or more, fueled by their own original ideas and rich use of language. We start to distinguish between the sound of a chaotic classroom and the hum of energy when children are deeply absorbed in the flow of play.

Young children work hard at play. They invent scenes and stories, solve problems, and negotiate their way through social roadblocks. They know what they want to do and work diligently to do it. Because their motivation comes from within, they learn the powerful lesson of pursuing their own ideas to a successful conclusion.

Research shows that children who engage in complex forms of socio-dramatic play have greater language skills than nonplayers, better social skills, more empathy, more imagination, and more of the subtle capacity to know what others mean. They are less aggressive and show more self-control and higher levels of thinking. Animal research suggests that they have larger brains with more complex neurological structures than nonplayers.

Long-term research casts doubt on the assumption that starting earlier on the teaching of phonics and other discrete skills leads to better results. For example, most of the play-based kindergartens in Germany were changed into centers for cognitive achievement during a wave of educational "reform" in the 1970s. But research comparing 50 play-based classes with 50 early-learning centers found that by age ten the children who had played excelled over the others in a host of ways. They were more advanced in reading and mathematics and they were better adjusted socially and emotionally in school. They excelled in creativity and intelligence, oral expression, and "industry."[*] As a result of this study German kindergartens returned to being play-based again.

---

[*]These findings are summarized in "Curriculum Studies and the Traditions of Inquiry: The Scientific Tradition" by Linda Darling-Hammond and Jon Snyder, in the *Handbook of Research on Curriculum* (1992), edited by Philip W. Jackson; New York: MacMillan, pp. 41-78.

China and Japan are envied in the U.S. for their success in teaching science, math, and technology. But one rarely hears about their approach to schooling before second grade, which is playful and experiential rather than didactic. Finland's children, too, go to playful kindergartens, and they enter first grade at age seven rather than six. They enjoy a lengthy, playful early childhood. Yet Finland consistently gets the highest scores on the respected international PISA exam for 15-year-olds.

It is true that poverty does not afflict Finland's children as it does children in the U.S., and that children of poverty need special attention in preschool and kindergarten. But what they need is extra support to reap the full benefits of a play-based, experiential program. They may need more structure to begin with and guidance for entering into play, for many are inexperienced with it. They need a solid introduction to books, which most middle-class children have from infancy onwards, and they need to hear language used in conversation, storytelling, song, and verse. Equally important, they need to use language. Play is the foremost way that children use the language they are hearing.

In an effective play-based kindergarten the teacher has a strong though subtle role. She understands child development—cognitive, physical, and social-emotional. The teacher is attuned to the children's play themes and builds on them, introducing new content and play materials to stimulate their minds. She knows the needs of individual children and helps them overcome obstacles in their lives that hinder learning. In other words, she is a well-trained professional who is part of a learning community where teachers support each other in their growth and where

administrators appreciate her work. She expects much from her children and knows how to create a classroom that supports excellence.

All young children, not just those living in poverty, need this kind of support. For the fact is that most children today don't have enough playtime even at home. Many affluent children now need help entering into creative play because of the surfeit of media and organized activities in their lives. They struggle to bring their own ideas to the fore. As one kindergarten teacher put it, "If I give the children time to play, they don't know what to do. They have no ideas of their own."

This is a tragedy, both for the children themselves and for our nation and world. No human being can achieve his full potential if his creativity is stunted in childhood. And no nation can thrive in the 21st century without a highly creative and innovative workforce. Nor will democracy survive without citizens who can form their own independent thoughts and act on them.

The power of play as the engine of learning in early childhood and as a vital force for young children's physical, social, and emotional development is beyond question. Children in play-based kindergartens have a double advantage over those who are denied play: they end up equally good or better at reading and other intellectual skills, and they are more likely to become well-adjusted healthy people.

Every child deserves a chance to grow and learn in a play-based, experiential preschool and kindergarten. Play works.

DAVID ELKIND

FOREWORD

EARLY CHILDHOOD EDUCATION, the care and instruction of young children outside of the home, over the last half century has become a downward extension of schooling. It is now the first rung on the educational ladder. In many respects, however, this most recent addition to the pedagogical hierarchy is quite different from its elementary and secondary predecessors.

The early childhood curriculum is the most holistic and least differentiated at any level of education. It is also the most solidly grounded in philosophy, in clearly articulated methodology, and in theory and research. Those who contributed to the discipline of early childhood education came from occupations and professions outside the academic domain. What they had in common was an understanding of children. And that is what makes early childhood education unique; it starts with the child and not with the subject matter.

The philosophical foundations of early childhood education were provided by John Amos Comenius, John Locke, and Jean Jacques Rousseau. Its curriculum and methodology were created by Johann Heinrich Pestalozzi, Friedrich Froebel, Maria Montessori, and Rudolf Steiner. Most recently it was scientifically grounded by the research and theory of Sigmund Freud, Jean Piaget, and Erik Erikson. While there are differences in the approaches of these progenitors of early childhood education, the differences are overshadowed by one common principle: *that young children are growing and that early childhood curriculum and practice have to be adapted to the maturing needs, abilities, and interests of the child.*

Today, however, as is made so heartbreakingly clear by the Alliance for Childhood report, the rich legacy of the grandmasters, supported by an overwhelming amount of contemporary research findings and classroom experience, is dismissed as irrelevant. Instead we have had a politically and commercially driven effort to make kindergarten a one-size-smaller first grade. Why in the world are we trying to teach the elementary curriculum at the early childhood level?

The answer, I am afraid, is that what we do in education has little or nothing to do with what we know is good pedagogy for children. For example, we could significantly improve education at all levels and in all parts of the country with one change in policy—reducing class size to 18 or less at all grade levels. It is a basic truism of education that the more one-on-one time a child has with a teacher, the better the learning and educational outcome. Yet in practice educational policy is determined by political, economic, cultural, and personal ego concerns. This happens because children and adolescents do not vote, and have little or no say in their own governance. And we, who speak for children and youth, have not been able to muster the political muscle to make the educational needs of children either heard or responded to.

The data and arguments offered in this report are both powerful and compelling. But if they are to have any impact, we need to find champions in the media, in the arts, and in politics who will make the case for us. After all, what do we know? We are just the teachers of young children—who just happen to be the future of our nation.

Crisis in the Kindergarten:
Why Children Need to Play in School

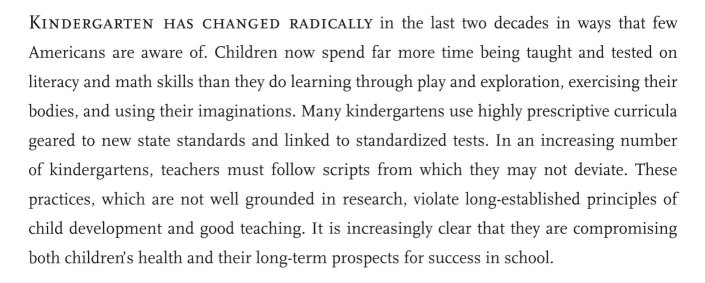

Kindergarten has changed radically in the last two decades in ways that few Americans are aware of. Children now spend far more time being taught and tested on literacy and math skills than they do learning through play and exploration, exercising their bodies, and using their imaginations. Many kindergartens use highly prescriptive curricula geared to new state standards and linked to standardized tests. In an increasing number of kindergartens, teachers must follow scripts from which they may not deviate. These practices, which are not well grounded in research, violate long-established principles of child development and good teaching. It is increasingly clear that they are compromising both children's health and their long-term prospects for success in school.

The traditional kindergarten classroom that most adults remember from childhood—with plenty of space and time for unstructured play and discovery, art and music, practicing social skills, and learning to enjoy learning—has largely disappeared. The latest research indicates that, on a typical day, children in all-day kindergartens spend four to six times as much time in literacy and math instruction and taking or preparing for tests (about two to three hours per day) as in free play or "choice time" (30 minutes or less).

Kindergartners are now under great pressure to meet inappropriate expectations, including academic standards that until recently were reserved for first grade. At the same time, they are being denied the benefits of play—a major stress reliever. This double burden, many experts believe, is contributing to a rise in anger and aggression in young children, reflected in increasing reports of severe behavior problems. Given the high rates of psychiatric disturbances among children today, it is critically important that early education practices

promote physical and emotional health and not exacerbate illness.

High-stakes testing and test preparation in kindergarten are proliferating, as schools increasingly are required to make decisions on promotion, retention, and placement in gifted programs or special education classes on the basis of test scores. While some testing of children under age eight may be useful for screening, it is a highly unreliable method for assessing individual children. Observational and curriculum-embedded performance assessments should be used instead. The argument that standardized testing takes less time and is therefore more efficient is called into question by new data suggesting that teachers are now spending 20 to 30 minutes per day preparing kindergarten children to take standardized tests.

The nine new studies and analyses on which this report is based all point to the same conclusion: kindergarten, long a beloved institution in American culture, is in crisis. If the problems are not recognized and remedied, the same ills will be passed on to preschools and even to programs for children ages birth to three.

The implications of these radical changes in early education practice reach far beyond schools. Until recently few people were talking about the long-term effects of the disappearance of children's play. Now, while many politicians and policymakers are calling for even more tests, more accountability, and more hard-core academics in early childhood classrooms, the leaders of major business corporations are saying that creativity and play are the future of the U.S. economy.

Daniel Pink, author of *A Whole New Mind*, writes about the "imagination economy," and says that "people have to be able to do something that can't be outsourced, something that's hard to automate and that delivers on the growing demand for nonmaterial things like stories and design. Typically these are things we associate with the right side of the brain, with artistic and empathetic and playful sorts of abilities." How can we expect our children to thrive in the imagination economy of the future if we deny them opportunities for play and creativity in kindergarten?

We recognize that the restoration of child-initiated play to early education will not by itself solve the complex problems of helping all children—especially those with special needs or in poor families and neglected schools, as well as English-language learners—to reach their full potential. We are not calling for a simple return to the practices of an earlier time. We now understand much better the kinds of rich experiences that young children need in order to become avid learners. Teachers need to understand the ways in which child-initiated play when combined with playful, focused learning leads to lifelong benefits in ways that didactic drills, standardized tests, and scripted teaching do not.

In a healthy kindergarten, play does not mean "anything goes." It does not deteriorate into chaos. Nor is play so tightly structured by adults that children are denied the opportunity to learn through their own initiative and exploration. Kindergartners need a balance of child-initiated play in the presence of engaged teachers and more focused experiential learning guided by teachers. We call for educators, their professional organizations, and policymakers to develop as fully as possible the two central methods in the continuum (illustrated below) of approaches to kindergarten education:

THE KINDERGARTEN CONTINUUM

Laissez-Faire, Loosely Structured Classroom	Classroom Rich in Child-Initiated Play	Playful Classroom with Focused Learning	Didactic, Highly Structured Classroom
Ample play but without active adult support, often resulting in chaos	Exploring the world through play with the active presence of teachers	Teachers guiding learning with rich, experiential activities	Teacher-led instruction, including scripted teaching, with little or no play

The creation of a healthy balance described above has been blocked by current policies and government-imposed practices and programs, including No Child Left Behind and Reading First. These well-intentioned but fundamentally flawed mandates rely on testing and on didactic and scripted approaches—especially for teaching children from low-income backgrounds—in spite of the fact that these practices are not well supported by research evidence. Indeed, many of the current approaches to kindergarten education are based on unfounded assumptions and preconceptions about what is best for children and schools.

"The problem is not *political* but *ideological*," writes Lilian Katz, who directed the ERIC Clearinghouse on Elementary and Early Childhood Education for 30 years. "Ideologies are deeply held beliefs that fill the vacuum created by the unavailability of hard data. Our best strategy in such situations is to make our ideas and the data that we do have readily available to others who can subject them to vigorous argument and debate."

If we are to best serve children and to foster the full professional development of early childhood educators, we must reject an ideological approach to teaching young children, consider all the evidence of decades of research and experience—not just the results of a few narrow tests of suspect validity—and begin a thorough reassessment of our kindergarten policies and practices.

Based on our reading of the evidence, we call on policymakers, educators, health professionals, researchers, and parents to take action as follows:

1. **Restore child-initiated play and experiential learning with the active support of teachers to their rightful place at the heart of kindergarten education.**

2. **Reassess kindergarten standards to ensure that they promote developmentally appropriate practices, and eliminate those that do not.**

3. **End the inappropriate use in kindergarten of standardized tests, which are prone to serious error especially when given to children under age eight.**

4. **Expand the early childhood research agenda to examine the long-term impact of current preschool and kindergarten practices on the development of children from diverse backgrounds.**

5. **Give teachers of young children first-rate preparation that emphasizes the full development of the child and the importance of play, nurtures children's innate love of learning, and supports teachers' own capacities for creativity, autonomy, and integrity.**

6. **Use the crisis of play's disappearance from kindergarten to rally organizations and individuals to create a national movement for play in schools and communities.**

Chapter 1

Introduction: Crisis in the Kindergarten

Too few Americans are aware of the radical changes in kindergarten practice in the last ten to twenty years. Children now spend far more time being instructed and tested in literacy and math than they do learning through play* and exploration, exercising their bodies, and using their imaginations. Many kindergartens use highly prescriptive curricula linked to standardized tests. An increasing number of teachers must follow scripts from which they may not deviate. Many children struggle to live up to academic standards that are developmentally inappropriate.

Such practices are contributing to high levels of frustration, stress, and anger in kindergartners, sometimes resulting in extreme behavior problems. At the same time that we have increased academic pressure in children's lives through inappropriate standards, we have managed to undermine their primary tool for dealing with stress—freely chosen, child-directed, intrinsically motivated play. David Elkind's "hurried child" is now not just hurried but also worried.

Early education at its best helps children strengthen their capacity for play and lays a strong foundation for a lifetime of growth and learning. There is an urgent need to transform the current emphasis in kindergartens on intensive training for short-term results to practices that support healthy development and produce lifelong learners. New approaches centered on child-initiated play and intentional teaching through play and hands-on learning are needed.

Play is one of the vital signs of health in children. We do not know the long-term consequences of the loss of play in early childhood, but this has become a concern for pediatricians and psychologists. In the absence of research on this critical question, we are blindly pursuing educational policies that could well damage the intellectual, social, and physical development of an entire generation.

With this report, containing important new empirical evidence of what is going on in our schools, the Alliance calls the attention of all Americans to a national disgrace: the transformation of public kindergartens from places where love of learning was thoughtfully nurtured into pressure-cooker classrooms where teachers are required to follow scripts, labor under unrealistic one-size-fits-all standards, and test children relentlessly on their performance. Kindergarten has ceased to be a garden of delight and has become a place of stress and distress.

For the purposes of this report, we use the word "play" to describe activities that are freely chosen and directed by children and arise from intrinsic motivation. Within this definition are many different kinds of play, including dramatic and make-believe play, block play, sand and water play, art activities, play with open-ended objects, spontaneous physical play, exploring the outdoors, and so on.

A Growing Awareness of the Early Education Crisis

During the past two decades child development experts and physicians have been alerting parents, educators, and policymakers about a looming crisis in early education caused by an alarming increase in didactic instruction and inappropriate testing, with a resulting decrease in play and experiential learning. It is these playful modes of learning that are much better suited to young children's growth and healthy development, rather than instruction calling for long periods of sedentary work.

"Our students spend most of the time trying to learn what they need in order to pass standardized testing," a kindergarten teacher in Los Angeles told researchers in 2008. "There is hardly enough time for activities like P.E, science, art, playtime."[1]

Beginning in 2001, the Alliance for Childhood issued three public warnings about the demise of play and the dangers of the dramatic increase in standardized testing mandated by the No Child Left Behind Act (NCLB). Dozens of eminent scholars, physicians, and education leaders have signed one or more of these statements, including T. Berry Brazelton, Robert Coles, Linda Darling-Hammond, David Elkind, Howard Gardner, Daniel Goleman, Stanley Greenspan, Jane Healy, and Alvin Poussaint.

In 2001 the Alliance wrote about the testing provisions of NCLB: "This massive experiment, intended to raise educational achievement, is based on misconceptions about the nature and value of testing and about how children develop a true love of learning."[2] In 2003 the Alliance drafted a statement for the U.S. Senate Committee on Health, Education, Labor, and Pensions that read, in part:

> The key to developing literacy—and all other skills—is to pace the learning so that it is consistent with the child's development, enabling him or her to succeed at the early stages. Ensure this initial success and the child's natural love of learning blooms. Doom him to failure in the beginning by making inappropriate demands and he may well be unable to overcome the resulting sense of inadequacy. This is especially true of children whose families are already under social and economic stress.[3]

Two years later the Alliance issued a Call to Action[4] about early education. It begins: "We are deeply concerned that current trends in early education, fueled by political pressure, are leading to an emphasis on unproven methods of academic instruction and unreliable standardized testing that can undermine learning and damage young children's healthy development." (For full statement see Appendix A.)

School Life Out of Balance

The traditional kindergarten classroom that most adults remember from childhood—with plenty of space and time for unstructured play and discovery, art and music, practicing social skills, and learning to enjoy learning—has largely disappeared. Among the findings of the latest research, described in Chapter 2, is that, on a typical school day, kindergartners spend four to six times as much time in literacy and numeracy instruction and taking tests or preparing to take them (about two to three hours per day) as in free play or "choice time" (30 minutes or less).

A California kindergarten teacher, commenting last year on the disappearance of blocks, told researchers, "I know how important they are, but the structure and intensity of the current kindergarten curriculum do not allow for much developmental activity."[5]

Achieving a healthy balance of activities in the classroom requires an understanding of kindergartners as emerging learners in literacy, math, and many other subjects. Their developing skills are supported by child-initiated play and by intentional teaching through play, art activities, and other hands-on experiences. Current pressure to teach literacy and math skills that used to be introduced in first or second grade has turned kindergarten into a highly structured and regimented ordeal in which the first lesson many children learn is that they're not good enough.

Most troubling in this hijacking of kindergarten is that there is no evidence that a heavy emphasis on teacher-led instruction and scripted curricula yields long-term benefits for children. In particular, low-income children who need support to succeed in school are not showing significant long-term gains.

Accountability must go beyond standardized test scores and look at gains and losses in children's overall physical and mental health.

Policymakers are overlooking the ample evidence that young children learn best in settings rich with warm human relationships, imaginative play, and playful learning, where children participate in choosing their activities and teachers help them build on their experiences—not following rigid curricula designed to increase test scores. Indeed, the testing mania that is now invading kindergarten is based on a false assumption—that standardized assessments are the best way to gauge young children's progress in school.

Nine New Studies Paint a Troubling Picture

Has the switch to a high-pressure academic model of kindergarten worked? Does scripted teaching and long hours of teacher-centered lessons enhance or diminish children's natural love of learning? In particular, are these methods serving the needs of young children most at risk of school failure?

The nine new studies and analyses on which this report is based focus on the role of play, child-initiated learning, highly structured curricula, and standardized testing. They all point to the same conclusion: kindergarten, long a beloved institution in American culture, is in serious trouble. If the problems are not recognized and remedied, the same ills will be passed on to preschools and even to programs for children ages birth to three.

Three of the studies were commissioned by the Alliance for Childhood and carried out by independent research teams at Long Island University, Sarah Lawrence College, and the University of California, Los Angeles. They looked at the current state of public school kindergartens in New York City, Westchester County (New York), and Los Angeles, with data collection completed in 2008. Two

research teams independently surveyed a total of 254 kindergarten teachers in New York City and Los Angeles; a third team made repeated in-depth observations in 14 kindergarten classrooms in the New York area and interviewed teachers and school principals.

This is the first research we know of in the United States that begins to create an accurate picture of how children spend their time in urban and suburban public kindergartens today, what materials are available to them, and the attitudes and beliefs of the adults who are charged with educating and caring for them. It is only a beginning. We strongly recommend that a comprehensive annual account of publicly funded programs in preschool and kindergarten be developed by the governments funding the programs. Accountability must go beyond standardized test scores and include gains and losses in children's overall physical and mental health. (See Chapter 8 for specific recommendations.)

The other six studies and analyses were conducted by a wide range of eminent researchers, including U.S. Department of Education evaluation experts, the American Academy of Pediatrics, the International Association for the Evaluation of Educational Achievement, the High/Scope Educational Research Foundation, and scholars from Yale University, Temple University, the University of Delaware, and Illinois State University.

The research on which this report is based follows:

A. Jennifer Astuto (Long Island University) and LaRue Allen (New York University) survey of 142 kindergarten teachers working in New York City using their Early Childhood Time-Use Scale (in preparation)

B. Allison Fuligni and Sandra Hong (U.C.L.A.) survey of 112 kindergarten teachers in Los Angeles using the Astuto-Allen Early Childhood Time-Use Scale (in preparation)

C. Sarah Lawrence College Child Development Institute study of 14 kindergarten classrooms in Westchester County, New York (in preparation)

D. Kathy Hirsh-Pasek, Roberta Michnick Golinkoff, Laura E. Berk, and Dorothy G. Singer, *A Mandate for Playful Learning in Preschool: Presenting the Evidence* (Oxford University Press, 2009)

E. Dorothy G. Singer, Jerome L. Singer, Heidi D'Agostino, and Raeka DeLong, "Children's Pastimes and Play in Sixteen Nations: Is Free-Play Declining?" *American Journal of Play*, Vol. 1, No. 3 (Winter 2008)[6]

F. U.S. Department of Education evaluation of Open Court Reading program (2008)[7]

G. U.S. Department of Education Reading First Impact Study, Final Report (2008)[8]

H. Kenneth R. Ginsburg et al., "The Importance of Play in Promoting Healthy Child Development and Maintaining Strong Parent-Child Bonds," *Pediatrics*, Vol. 119, No. 1 (January 2007)[9]

I. International Association for the Evaluation of Educational Achievement (IEA) and High/Scope Educational Research Foundation Preprimary Study Age-Seven Follow-up (2007).[10]

> **Open-ended play is now a minor activity, or has been completely eliminated, in the kindergartens studied.**

The Findings

These nine studies and analyses, all published within the past two years or still in the final stages of preparation for publication, reveal the following findings:

A preponderance of time in a sample of 254 New York City and Los Angeles kindergartens is devoted to teaching literacy and numeracy, and to testing and test preparation.

1. Play in all its forms, but especially open-ended child-initiated play, is now a minor activity, if not completely eliminated, in the kindergartens assessed. Teacher-directed activities, especially instruction in literacy and math, are taking up the lion's share of classroom time. Standardized testing and preparation for tests are now a daily activity in most of these kindergartens. (From the studies labeled A and B in the list above.)

2. Most teachers in the two new studies of New York City and Los Angeles kindergartens say they spend two to three hours each day in literacy, math, and test prep—and that children have 30 minutes or less each day for play or "choice time." (A, B)

3. In Los Angeles, 25 percent of the teachers surveyed said there was no time at all for free play in their kindergartens. (B)

4. There is apparently a wide divergence in what educators mean by "play." Most of the activities that are set up in "choice time" or "center time," and are described as play by some teachers, are in fact teacher-directed and involve little or no free play, imagination, or creativity. (C)

Preschool and kindergarten children benefit from play and playful learning, from choosing their own activities, and from individual and small-group pursuits rather than whole-group ones.

5. A review of the research on how young children learn by four eminent scholars of early childhood concludes that "children need both unstructured free play and playful learning under the gentle guidance of adults to best prepare them for entrance into formal school; academic and social development are

Standardized testing has become an established part of kindergarten in spite of serious doubts about its validity in early childhood.

so inextricably intertwined that the former must not trump attention to the latter; and ... learning takes place best when children are engaged and enjoying themselves." (D)

6. The American Academy of Pediatrics issued a major clinical report concluding that "play is essential to development. ... Play allows children to use their creativity while developing their imagination, dexterity, and physical, cognitive, and emotional strength. Play is important to healthy brain development. It is through play that children at a very early age engage and interact in the world around them. Play allows children to create and explore a world they can master, conquering their fears while practicing adult roles, sometimes in conjunction with other children or adult caregivers. As they master their world, play helps children develop new competencies that lead to enhanced confidence and the resiliency they will need to face future challenges. Undirected play allows children to learn how to work in groups, to share, to negotiate, to resolve conflicts, and to learn self-advocacy skills." (H)

7. A new review of research by Jerome Singer and Dorothy Singer of Yale University concludes that make-believe play helps children "(a) expand vocabulary and link objects with actions, (b) develop object constancy, (c) form event schemas and scripts, (d) learn strategies for problem-solving, (e) develop divergent thinking ability, and (f) develop a flexibility in shifting between different types of thought (narrative and logical)." (E)

8. A cross-national study of more than 1,500 young children in ten countries found that in every country children's language performance at age seven improved when teachers let children choose their activities rather than impose didactic lessons. (I)

9. The same international study found that young children's cognitive performance at age seven improved when children spent less time in whole-group activities and more time working or playing individually or in small groups. (I)

A sample of kindergarten teachers in New York City and Los Angeles report that imaginative and dramatic play is disappearing because of lack of materials and funding, lack of support from school administrators, and curricula that don't allow for such activities.

10. Dramatic make-believe play, essential for young children's development of literacy, social skills, and imagination, is limited by lack of materials. In both New York and L.A. only 12 to 13 percent of the teachers surveyed said they had enough dramatic play materials for all the children. (A, B)

11. Teachers in both New York and L.A. consistently reported that major factors working against dramatic play, block play, use of open-ended objects, and artistic activities in their kindergartens were that the curriculum doesn't incorporate those activities, there was not enough time for them, and school administrators did not value them. (A, B)

12. New York and L.A. teachers consistently reported major differences between their views of the importance of dramatic play, block play, and sand and water play and their perception of the views of school administrators. A large majority of teachers indicated that such play is important, while roughly half of the teachers perceived administrators as not valuing it. (A, B)

The pervasive use of standardized tests to measure children's progress in literacy and math has become an established part of kindergarten education in spite of a consensus among educational testing professionals that the results of such testing of children under age eight are subject to serious errors and their use is largely invalid.

13. Seventy-nine percent of the New York teachers surveyed reported spending time every day in testing or test preparation. In Los Angeles, it was 82 percent. Many of the teachers said they spend more than 30 minutes per day in these activities. (A, B)

Scripted teaching and other highly didactic types of curricula are widely used in kindergartens despite a lack of scientific evidence that they yield long-term gains.

14. Almost all of the L.A. teachers surveyed used McGraw-Hill's Open Court Reading, a scripted curriculum with highly regimented drills and exercises. But a new report from the U.S. Department of Education's Institute of Education Sciences finds that there are no valid studies showing that Open Court works, in spite of initial claims by the government that it is "research-based." (F)

15. A separate evaluation commissioned by the Institute of Education Sciences found that the federal government's Reading First program had significantly increased (by about 20%) the amount of class time spent on didactic, phonics-heavy reading instruction; nevertheless, the program "did not have statistically significant impacts on student reading comprehension test scores in grades 1–3." The evaluation also found that the program actually reduced second-grade students' engagement in reading and writing. (G)

The push for more academics in early education has reduced time for unstructured play, even as mothers and pediatricians have grown deeply concerned about its demise.

16. A new cross-cultural research study—by Jerome Singer and Dorothy Singer of Yale University—of 2,400 mothers in 16 countries found that, overall, 72 percent believe that children are "growing up too quickly." In the U.S., the figure is 95 percent, the highest of any country studied. (E)

17. The authors of this same study conclude that "mothers are deeply concerned that their youngsters are somehow missing out on the joys and experiential learning opportunities of free play and natural exploration. ... For lack of safe outdoor play spaces, and unstructured free time, children are being deprived of the excitement and social interactions of a healthy youth." (E)

18. The American Academy of Pediatrics, in its clinical report on the importance of play, found that "despite the benefits derived from play for both children and parents, time for free play has been markedly reduced for some children" and addressed "a variety of factors that have reduced play, including a hurried lifestyle, changes in family structure, and increased attention to academics and enrichment activities at the expense of recess or free child-centered play." (H)

The urge to play is still alive in children and needs to be nurtured.

19. In spite of dwindling time and materials for dramatic and imaginative play in many kindergartens, children's innate playfulness is irrepressible, like a plant pushing up through a crack in concrete. Sarah Lawrence College researchers found that, given the slightest opportunity, many children seize the moment to create imaginative play episodes. (C)

Scripted and Didactic Teaching: Suspect Methods Promoted Under NCLB

Despite publishers' claims that scripted teaching and similar didactic approaches are "research-based," there is little or no research showing long-term gains in reading skills or enjoyment of reading from these programs, and no evidence of short-term gains in comprehension. We know from research by the High/Scope Educational Research Foundation that short-term increases in test scores resulting from these practices tend to disappear after a few years. Yet short-term test-score gains in first and second grades get prominent coverage in the news media, while parents are not informed of the lack of long-term gains or of the risks associated with didactic, test-driven practices.

The High/Scope Preschool Curriculum Comparison Study, which followed the students' progress through age 23, showed that at-risk preschoolers required more treatment for emotional problems and ultimately committed more felonies if they were taught in a scripted curriculum classroom rather than a play-based program.

Overall, the children who experienced the High/Scope curriculum or the traditional nursery school approach, both of which "emphasized child-initiated activities in which young children pursued their own interests with staff support," did better than students in the Direct Instruction or scripted program on a total of 17 variables. At age 23, for instance, the former High/Scope and traditional nursery students aspired to complete a higher level of education and lived with spouses in greater numbers than the former Direct Instruction students. High/Scope concludes: "It thus appears that preschool programs that promote child-initiated activities (such as the High/Scope and Nursery School programs) seem to contribute to the development of an individual's sense of personal and social responsibility." [11]

The High/Scope study raised red flags about scripted teaching, and interest in the approach declined. Yet this unproved and potentially destructive method has seen a rapid comeback in part because urban schools are desperately seeking ways to help children from low-income families and other at-risk students to catch up with more privileged students. This is a vitally important goal, but the methods being used are often seriously flawed. The approved list of curricula issued by the federal Reading First program was heavy with scripted and other highly structured approaches. But recent research by the Government Accountability Office found that favoritism and conflicts of interest corrupted the process of choosing kindergarten curricula, "especially among researchers who had developed reading-instruction products that would profit from the program's bounty." [12]

The latest data on outcomes of Reading First programs have cast serious doubts on the efficacy of the curricula selected by the federal government. The government's own evaluators found that the so-called research-based approaches did not improve reading comprehension despite the fact that schools were spending more time teaching the five core literacy activities demanded by Reading First. Funds have been cut back for Reading First and its future is at present endangered. The pity of this is that children from low-income homes often do need extra support to become skilled and avid readers, and appropriate methods exist—but they are not the approaches favored under NCLB.

A new study found that mothers are deeply concerned that their children are missing out on the joys of free play and natural exploration.

An Urgent Need for Action

The combined import of these new studies calls for immediate concerted action. The situation is urgent.

Twenty years ago a North Carolina study found that kindergarten teachers felt their students were under significant stress from an increasingly academic curriculum. [13] Today there are mounting reports of stressed-out kindergartners, behavior problems including uncontrollable anger and aggression, and expulsion of young children from school, a problem that is particularly severe for young boys.

A Connecticut school official attributed a spike in violence among young children in 2007 to the increasing emphasis on standardized testing and the elimination of time for recess, gym, and other chances to play. "It's not like it was when we were kids, when you could expect to have an hour or so every day to play and explore," she said. "That kind of time just isn't there anymore." [14]

Clinical research on the links between play deprivation, stress levels, and related health and behavioral problems in kindergarten children is sorely lacking. But many experts believe that developmentally inappropriate expectations and practices are causing normal child behavior to be wrongly labeled as misbehavior, and normal learning patterns to be mislabeled as learning disabilities. "This early and inappropriate labeling may have lifelong implications for children who are developing their self-image," says pediatrician Kenneth R. Ginsburg of the Children's Hospital of Philadelphia and lead author of the *Pediatrics* report on play. "Further, labels travel with children and may flavor future teachers' and even caregivers' assessments and interactions."

THE KINDERGARTEN CONTINUUM

Laissez-Faire, Loosely Structured Classroom	Classroom Rich in Child-Initiated Play	Playful Classroom with Focused Learning	Didactic, Highly Structured Classroom
Ample play but without active adult support, often resulting in chaos	Exploring the world through play with the active presence of teachers	Teachers guiding learning with rich, experiential activities	Teacher-led instruction, including scripted teaching, with little or no play

For the health of the children and their long-term success in school and in life, a better approach to kindergarten is needed, one that allows children and their teachers to learn and work in an atmosphere that encourages exploration and creativity and lays a strong foundation for emerging literacy, numeracy, and other vital capacities. Such approaches, when combined with the active presence of teachers who understand child-initiated play and learning and know how to create a rich environment for them, allow kindergartens to support children's healthy development and enhance and extend their knowledge.

In a healthy kindergarten, play does not mean "anything goes." The laissez-faire classroom, in which the teacher sits back and provides little structure and few boundaries, may abound in children's play, but it is often superficial and chaotic. At the other extreme, kindergarten should not be so tightly structured that children are denied

> "Inappropriate labeling may have lifelong implications for children who are developing their self-image." —DR. KENNETH GINSBURG

opportunities to learn through their own initiative and exploration. Kindergartners need a balance of child-initiated play in the presence of engaged teachers with more focused experiential learning activities led by teachers.

This range of kindergarten education is illustrated in the continuum above. We call for educators, their professional organizations, and policymakers to develop as fully as possible the two central methods in the continuum: child-initiated play and focused, experiential learning.

The dangers of the extremes in early education are described by researchers Elena Bodrova and Deborah Leong: "In our experiences, we have found that both extremely chaotic classrooms and extremely teacher-directed classrooms are counterproductive to developing self-regulation and other underlying skills in children. Classrooms where children flit from activity to activity support reactive behavior. But when all the instruction is whole-group, students become too teacher-regulated."[15]

In Chapter 7 we offer specific information for educators and policymakers who want to create more playful kindergartens and schools. In Chapter 8 we summarize the most critical findings of this report and provide a comprehensive list of recommendations for action by policymakers, school administrators, teachers, and parents who are alarmed by what is happening to so many of our children and want to create healthy, balanced kindergartens for them.

Chapter 2

The Transformation of Kindergarten

New evidence from research shows that didactic instruction and testing are pushing play out of kindergarten. Kindergartners are now under intense pressure to meet inappropriate expectations, including academic standards that until recently were reserved for first or second grade. These expectations and the policies that result from them have greatly reduced and in some cases obliterated opportunities for imaginative, child-initiated play in kindergarten.

The evidence from the three new studies described in this chapter suggests that public school kindergarten education is now very different from what most adults recall from their own childhoods. We do not have comparative data from the past on the amounts of time and materials for play that earlier generations of kindergartners enjoyed. We do, however, have the direct observations of early childhood educators and researchers—and they are alarmed.

Professor Nancy Carlsson-Paige of Lesley University has taught, supervised teachers, and conducted research in kindergartens for more than 30 years, working in both urban and suburban schools. "The loss of play and child-centered learning that these new studies reveal signals great cause for concern," she says. "Decades of research and theory in child development affirm the importance of play in the early years as the primary vehicle through which children build a strong foundation for cognitive, social, and emotional concepts. The loss of this foundation that can only be built through play will undermine children's success in school and academic competence for years to come."

The data from these new studies, combined with her own observations, "show clearly that the kindergartens of today barely resemble those I visited fifteen years ago," says Carlsson-Paige. "The majority of children today are spending most of their time in teacher-directed activities, especially in literacy and math, and have little time for activities of their choice. The vast majority of kindergarten teachers now spend some time each day on testing and test preparation, an activity that would have been considered irrelevant and even harmful in the past."

"Across all of my experiences in classrooms," says Carlsson-Paige, describing the kindergartens of a generation ago, "no matter what school I was visiting—whether it used a traditional or a progressive pedagogy, whether it was public or private—I found consistency among kindergartens. Without exception, there was an emphasis on play and hands-on learning in kindergarten. In the classrooms I visited, children would choose the area they wanted to go to each day to start out, and then choose other areas as the day went on. Sometimes teachers would

Rich dramatic and make-believe play is rarely seen in today's schools.

encourage certain children to explore specific areas, and sometimes teachers asked that all children spend some time in a particular area, such as the literacy area. But the emphasis was always on choices made by children. Most of the school day was spent in active, child-centered, imaginative exploration and play."

> ## "Many teachers don't know the reasons why play is important."
>
> —DIANE LEVIN

Professor Diane Levin of Wheelock College, another long-time kindergarten researcher, confirms these observations, noting that school principals "are under much more pressure now to push formal academics in kindergarten." For a variety of reasons, she says, rich dramatic and make-believe play is rarely seen in today's schools. "Play is not completely gone, but it is often superficial," she says, adding that many children still show playful behavior but are not able to develop complex play scenarios for extended periods.

Confirming the findings of the qualitative study (see below), Levin adds that in her own research she finds that today's teachers "may say that play is important, but they often don't recognize the difference between the imitative, repetitive play frequently seen today and the more creative, elaborated play of the past. Many teachers don't know the reasons why play is important. And now it's even more important for them to be able to articulate those reasons, and to understand why play is not happening in their classrooms—including the fact that screen time and other changes at home can undermine children's ability to engage in creative play without teachers' help."

We recognize that the restoration of child-initiated play to early education will not by itself solve the complex problems of helping all children—especially those with special needs or in poor families and neglected schools, as well as English-language learners—to reach their full potential. We are not calling for a simple return to the practices of an earlier time. We now understand much better the kinds of rich language experiences and skills that young children need in order to become literate, avid learners. Teachers need to understand the ways in which child-initiated play when combined with playful, intentional teaching leads to lifelong benefits in ways that didactic drills, standardized tests, and scripted teaching do not.

Play is a major mode for learning in early childhood. With sensible boundaries and support from teachers, it leads to enormous growth in all aspects of the child's development—cognitive, social, emotional, imaginative, and physical. Furthermore, it is the primary tool through which children explore their interests, express their joys, and process their fears, disappointments, and sorrows.

"The research is clear," says Nancy Carlsson-Paige. "Faster is not better when it comes to early education; young children need play and hands-on interactions for genuine learning to occur. We must reverse this destructive trend and develop education policies that are grounded in research and theory in child development and early childhood education."

> ## "Faster is not better when it comes to early education."
>
> —NANCY CARLSSON-PAIGE

Background of the Studies and Summary of Findings

The three university research studies described below, commissioned by the Alliance for Childhood and completed in 2008, provide clear evidence of the endangered status of child-initiated play in public school kindergartens in New York City and Westchester County, New York, and Los Angeles, California.

Two research teams, from Long Island University[*] and U.C.L.A.,[†] surveyed a total of 254 teachers in full-day kindergartens in New York and Los Angeles—the quantitative studies. A third team, from Sarah Lawrence College,[‡] made repeated in-depth observations in 14 kindergarten classrooms in New York and interviewed teachers and school principals—the qualitative study.

These studies were designed to help create an accurate picture of how children spend their time in public kindergartens today, what materials are available to them, and the attitudes and beliefs of the adults who are charged with educating and caring for them. Detailed findings of these studies are available on the Alliance for Childhood web site: www.allianceforchildhood.org.

In brief, the findings of these three studies suggest that:

- Teacher-directed activities, especially instruction in literacy and math skills, are taking up the lion's share of kindergarten classroom time.

- Standardized testing and preparation for tests are now a daily activity in most of the kindergartens studied.

- Free play, or "choice time," is usually limited to 30 minutes or less per day. In many classrooms there is no playtime at all.

> Teachers mean very different things by "play"—and often it is not play at all.

- Most classrooms do not have enough materials for all children to engage in play at once; blocks, dramatic play materials, and sand and water for play and exploration are in particularly short supply.

- Teachers say that major obstacles to play in kindergarten are that the curriculum does not incorporate it, that there is not enough time, and that administrators do not value it.

- Most teachers say that play in kindergarten is important, although few teachers or administrators are able to articulate the relationship between play and learning.

- There are wide variations in what teachers and principals mean by "play."

- Many classroom activities that adults describe as play are in fact highly teacher-directed and involve little or no imagination or creativity on the part of children.

[*] Jennifer Astuto of Long Island University and the Child and Family Policy Center at New York University (jennifer.astuto@nyu.edu) developed the Early Childhood Time-Use Scale used in both New York and Los Angeles and was lead researcher in the New York City study in collaboration with LaRue Allen of New York University.

[†] The U.C.L.A. researchers were Allison Fuligni (afulign@exchange.calstatela.edu) and Sandra Hong (sandyhong@ucla.edu) of the Center for Improving Child Care Quality, which is directed by Carollee Howes.

[‡] The Sarah Lawrence College research team was directed by Jan Drucker (jdrucker@slc.edu), Margery Franklin (mbf@slc.edu), and Barbara Schecter (schecter@slc.edu) of the college's Child Development Institute.

The Qualitative Study

The Sarah Lawrence study looked at 14 kindergarten classrooms in six urban and suburban communities in Westchester County, New York. The principals and teachers interviewed by the researchers included a wide range of activities in their definitions of play, including teacher-organized activities such as planting a garden, organized games, and recess, as well as child-initiated free play. Their responses to questions like "What do you see as the role of play in kindergarten?," "What kinds of play take place in kindergarten?," and "How is play related to learning?" similarly evinced a wide range of opinions, from a view of play as separate from learning (and incidental to it), to a view that play is integral to learning.

The Sarah Lawrence research team summarized their findings as follows:

1. *What principals and teachers mean by "play" varies.* They generally did not distinguish imaginative play from other activities that include manipulative materials, games, gardens, and centers. Most teachers referred to "free choice time" or "center time," and did not actually call this "play." They often did not bring up the topic of play in the context of questions about free choice time until the researchers brought it up. Principals and teachers in the same school often differed in how they talked about play—in emphasis, allotment of time, priority, urgency, and degree of conflict with other activities.

2. *The relationship of play to learning was rarely articulated* by principals or teachers.

3. Even when teachers and principals said they thought play is important, or that play leads to learning, they were usually referring to *an understanding of play as a highly scripted, teacher-directed activity.*

4. *The amount of choice time or center time in the 14 classrooms varied* from as little as 30 minutes once every 6 days to one hour every day. The great majority of classrooms had choice or center time every day.

> **The degree of actual free choice that children had during "choice time" varied from ample to none.**

Two classrooms provided less than 30 minutes of choice or center time, and only one provided 60 minutes (2 sessions of 30 minutes each), with the majority having 30 minutes. Taking into account the time for getting started and for clean-up, the actual time for children's activities was less than the allotted time, sometimes considerably so.

5. *The materials available to children at centers in different classrooms varied greatly,* from a well-stocked housekeeping corner to a barely furnished one; from good-sized collections of blocks to very few blocks.

6. *The degree of actual free choice that children were given during choice time varied* from ample (all materials in the room were available to all children in six of the classrooms) to none in one classroom (the children were assigned to centers by the teacher).

7. *The variation in play in different classrooms seemed to be the result of a complex interaction of factors,* including the larger educational culture, government mandates, and the views, values, and interests of individual educators in administrative and instructional positions within schools.

The researchers also noted this observation: "Even given restricted choices, little equipment, and inadequate amounts of time, children seize the moment to create imaginative play episodes." How these children would do if given more time to develop complex play scenarios is not known, but it was encouraging to see that the spark of play was still there despite all the obstacles.

The Quantitative Studies

Demographics and School Characteristics

In New York City, 142 teachers responded to the survey; in Los Angeles, 112 teachers responded—for a total of 254. All taught in full-day kindergartens.

In New York, 58% of the respondents had a master's degree. In L.A., 36% had a master's degree.

One-third of the Los Angeles teachers (34%) had not taken any courses in child development or early childhood education.

In New York, 51% of the respondents said they taught in Title I (high poverty) schools; 82% reported having at least four-fifths of their students on free lunch.

In Los Angeles 57% reported that they worked in Title I schools "in need of improvement"; 75% of the students received free lunch, while 60% were English-language learners.

McGraw-Hill's Open Court Reading curriculum was used by 88% of the Los Angeles teachers; 90% used either Harcourt Math or Scott Foresman Math. Most of the teachers (75%) in the New York City study reported using a curriculum offered through professional development workshops conducted by the Teachers College Reading and Writing Project at Columbia University.

How Kindergarten Children Spend Their Time in School

In both N.Y. and L.A. teachers reported spending much more time in teacher-directed instruction, especially of literacy and math skills, testing, and test preparation, than they gave children for free play or choice time.

Three-fourths of the New York City teachers (76%) spent more than an hour per day in literacy instruction. Almost one-fourth of them (23%) had more than an hour of daily math instruction. Only 2% reported giving students more than an hour of choice time per day. The average amount of daily choice time, calculated by using a weighted average of the teachers' reports, was 29.2 minutes. Almost four-fifths of the teachers (79%) reported spending some time on testing or test preparation on a typical day; 37% spent more than 30 minutes per day in test-related activities. 86% of the teachers reported that their classes had access to outdoor recess, weather permitting.

The results in Los Angeles were similar to the New York data: more than nine out of ten (92%) of the teachers said they spent more than an hour a day in literacy instruction; 17% had more than an hour of daily math instruction. Almost none gave children more than an hour of free play or choice time. The average amount of daily choice time was 19.1 minutes. One in four Los Angeles teachers said there was no time at all for "free play," although it is not clear how they differentiate free play from choice time. 97% of the teachers reported that their classes had access to outdoor recess, weather permitting.

TABLE 1: **Use of Kindergarten Classroom Time on a Typical Day, New York City**

	No time	1–30 min.	31–60 min.	61–90 min.	90+ min.	Total
Literacy instruction	0%	2%	22%	42%	34%	100%
Math instruction	0%	16%	61%	21%	2%	100%
Testing and test prep	21%	42%	28%	6%	3%	100%
Choice time	6%	54%	37%	1%	1%	99%

Note: Totals may not add up to 100% because of rounding.

TABLE 2: **Use of Kindergarten Classroom Time on a Typical Day, Los Angeles**

	No time	**1–30 min.**	**31–60 min.**	**61–90 min.**	**90+ min.**	Total
Literacy instruction	0%	1%	7%	31%	62%	101%
Math instruction	0%	13%	70%	17%	0%	100%
Testing and test prep	18%	63%	14%	3%	3%	101%
Choice time	13%	68%	18%	1%	0%	100%
Free play*	25%	54%	17%	4%	0%	100%

Note: Totals may not add up to 100% because of rounding.

*In Los Angeles only, teachers were asked about both "choice time" and "free play."

CHART A: **Daily Kindergarten Schedule in Two Cities** Average number of minutes spent daily in selected activities

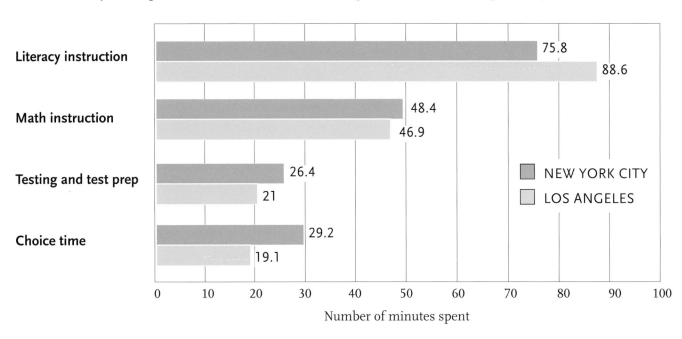

Availability of Kindergarten Classroom Materials

Dramatic play in the kindergartens surveyed is severely limited by lack of materials. In both New York and Los Angeles, only 12% to 13% of the teachers surveyed said their classrooms had enough dramatic play materials for all children to use at the same time. More than half the teachers reported not having enough materials for even half the class to use them at the same time. Sand or water play is nonexistent in four out of five classrooms in both New York and Los Angeles, according to the teachers' reports. Art supplies and open-ended objects (such as manipulatives, bottle caps, string, pipe cleaners) were more commonly available than other play-related materials. Most available of all the materials listed in the survey were instructional or published materials (such as flashcards, workbooks, and textbooks).

TABLE 3: **Availability of Kindergarten Classroom Materials, New York City**

	None	For 1–2 children	For half of the children	For most of the children	For all the children	Total
Blocks	6%	36%	41%	11%	6%	100%
Dramatic play materials	13%	39%	35%	8%	5%	100%
Art supplies	2%	5%	8%	20%	65%	100%
Open-ended objects	2%	1%	25%	21%	52%	101%
Instructional materials	5%	5%	6%	20%	64%	100%

TABLE 4: **Availability of Kindergarten Classroom Materials, Los Angeles**

	None	For 1–2 children	For half of the children	For most of the children	For all the children	Total
Blocks*	18%	--	--	--	--	--
Dramatic play materials	32%	32%	24%	8%	4%	100%
Art supplies	2%	3%	8%	14%	73%	100%
Open-ended objects	6%	1%	16%	19%	59%	101%
Instructional materials	0%	2%	2%	7%	89%	100%

Totals may not add up to 100% because of rounding.

*Los Angeles teachers were asked about the number of blocks in their classrooms rather than how many children could play with them at once. 35% reported having more than 100 blocks. 46% reported having 50 or fewer. 18% said they had no blocks at all.

Use of blocks: 27% of the teachers reported that blocks were used daily in their kindergartens; 26% said they were used once a week; 20% said they were never used.

CHART B: **Classroom Materials in Two Cities** Enough materials for most or all children?

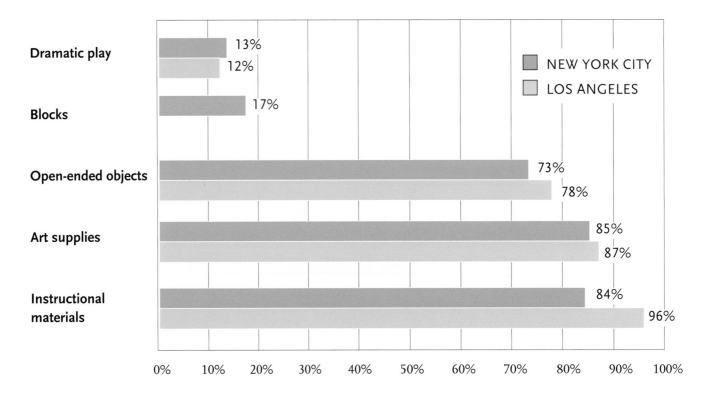

In Chart B above, figures "for most of the children" and "for all children" from Tables 3 and 4 above are combined.

Approximately four out of five classrooms in both the New York and Los Angeles samples did not provide sand or water tables for children's use, even though large majorities of the teachers believe such play is important for kindergarten children (see teachers' views below).

What Are the Obstacles to Play and Playful Learning in Kindergarten?

Teachers were asked to identify the obstacles to play in kindergarten. They consistently reported that among the main factors working against more opportunities

for dramatic play, block play, sand and water play, use of open-ended objects, and artistic activities in kindergarten classrooms was that the prescribed curriculum doesn't incorporate them. Other significant obstacles were lack of time, space, and funding.

When asked to identify the reasons why playful and creative activities were not present in some kindergartens, teachers consistently reported a conflict between their views and their perception of school administrators' views about the importance of dramatic play, block play, and sand and water play. Very few teachers said they believed that these activities were not important in kindergarten; roughly half of the teachers said they perceived the administration as not valuing them.

CHART C: **Obstacles to Kindergarten Play, New York City**

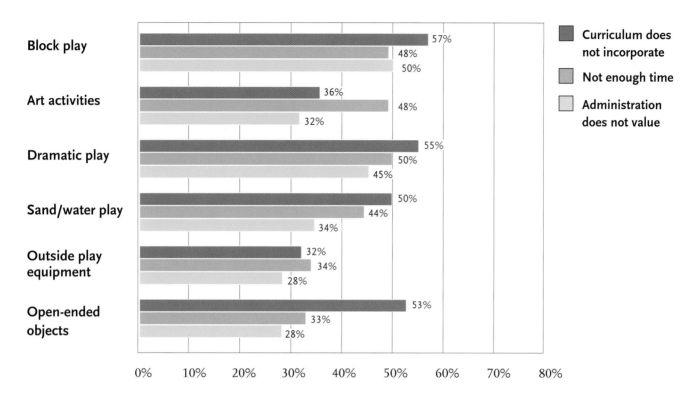

CHART D: **Obstacles to Kindergarten Play, Los Angeles**

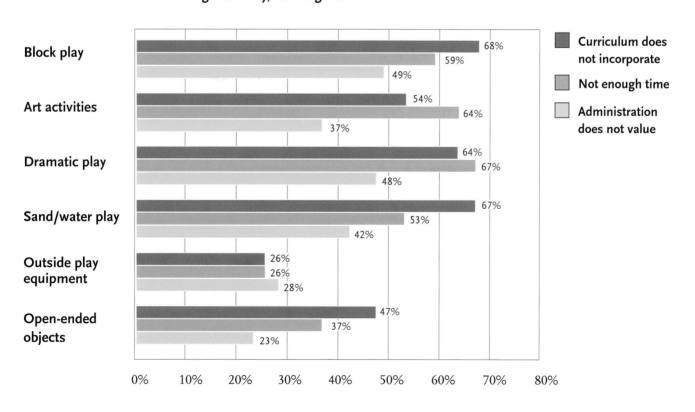

CHART E: **Perceived Importance of Playful and Creative Activities**

Teachers' views vs. perceived administration views

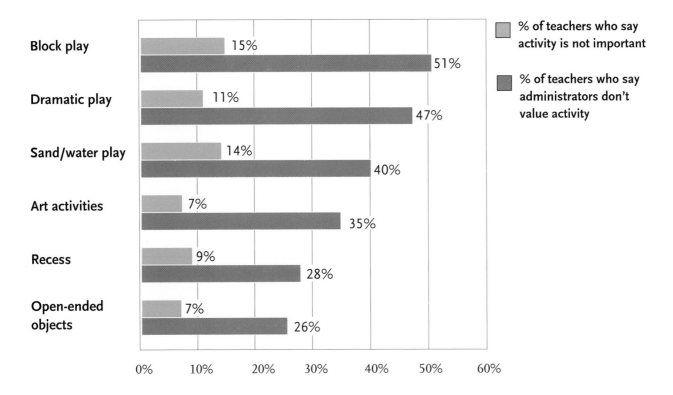

% of teachers who say activity is not important

% of teachers who say administrators don't value activity

Activity	% not important	% administrators don't value
Block play	15%	51%
Dramatic play	11%	47%
Sand/water play	14%	40%
Art activities	7%	35%
Recess	9%	28%
Open-ended objects	7%	26%

Conclusions

The research studies described in this chapter, because of their relatively limited scope, are strongly suggestive but not definitive. What they suggest is a crisis that calls for action—the restoration in kindergarten of play and playful learning, methods that have been shown to support healthy development and long-term gains in learning. Given the seriousness of the situation and its implications for the future, it is shocking that research on the loss of play and playful learning in kindergarten has until now simply not existed.

Among the recommendations listed in Chapter 8 of this report are that the federal government fund the replication on a much larger scale of the quantitative studies described above so that a representative sample of teachers in many different areas contribute to the full picture of current kindergarten practices. In this way trends can be monitored and guidelines or policies can be developed. In addition, well-designed longitudinal studies are needed that compare the outcomes of rich play-based approaches in kindergarten education with the outcomes of other methods, including those with a heavy emphasis on didactic instruction.

CHAPTER 3

REASSESSING STANDARDS: THE NEED FOR REALISTIC GUIDELINES

AT THE HEART OF GOOD EDUCATION is the art and science of matching adult expectations for children's achievements with the child's own ability to reach these goals in healthy ways. Unfortunately there is today a significant gap between what the standards dictate and what developmental experts recommend for kindergarten children.

With a new Administration in Washington and an upcoming debate on the reauthorization of the No Child Left Behind Act, it is helpful to recall *A Nation at Risk*, the 1983 document that helped shape contemporary American education. Its primary message was that American education had become moribund. "If an unfriendly foreign power had attempted to impose on America the mediocre educational performance that exists today," its authors famously wrote, "we might well have viewed it as an act of war." [16]

A Nation at Risk focused on the reform of high schools so that students would be better prepared for college and the workplace. It made recommendations in four major areas: content, standards, time, and teaching. Regarding standards, the report said: "We recommend that schools, colleges, and universities adopt more rigorous and measurable standards, and higher expectations, for academic performance and student conduct, and that

A Nation at Risk promoted high-school standards. No one foresaw that 25 years later kindergarten education would be dictated by standards.

4-year colleges and universities raise their requirements for admission. This will help students do their best educationally with challenging materials in an environment that supports learning and authentic accomplishment."

It is unlikely that anyone in 1983 foresaw the long-term effects of these recommendations, or of other changes in society like the growth of nursery schools and child care centers, on the lives of young children 25 years later: a radical shift of focus in their education.

Middle-class parents wanted their children to excel; at the same time, there was growing concern that children from low-income homes were lagging behind. Both sides came to the same conclusion: play was just a waste of time. Vivian Gussin Paley writes of this period in the history of kindergarten:

> The principles of child development were being rewritten, unaccompanied by a huge outcry of disbelief. One began to hear the word "boredom" attached to play, probably for the first time in human history. It was an odd concept to tag on to the single activity children loved best, but there was a growing nervousness about what was going on (or not going on) in kindergarten. The "academic kindergarten" was offered as the antidote to boredom and, further confusing our logic and commonsense, children labeled "at risk," who often had less opportunity for play and talk at home, were allowed less time for these activities at school as well. [17]

A Developmental Approach to Literacy

It is easiest to see the gulf between adult expectations and the realities of children's development in the area of literacy, which has been the subject of much research and public concern. The differences between normal expectations of emergent readers and some state standards are notable. Even when the differences are not great, the sheer number of standards in place, and the fact that they are no longer guidelines but strict requirements, has forced the American kindergarten to become the new first grade.

One of the best descriptions of how literacy develops in children between ages three and eight comes from the Bank Street College of Education in New York, a highly regarded institution for the study of early childhood.[18] The Bank Street guidelines differentiate between three main stages of literacy development from preschool to third grade. In summary, they are:

A. *Emergent readers and writers:* pre-kindergarten to first grade;

B. *Early readers:* first and second grades;

C. *Early fluent/fluent readers:* second and third grades.

While the Bank Street guidelines point out that children develop literacy in somewhat different ways and with different timetables, they describe kindergarten children, in general, as being *emergent readers and writers* rather than *early readers.* This is very different from today's prevailing expectations that children will become early readers and writers in kindergarten. The Bank Street approach enables kindergarten children to develop a foundation for literacy without straining to meet inappropriate demands.

According to Bank Street's guidelines, emergent readers and writers

- Understand that written language conveys messages

- Pretend read and write: they turn pages of books, invent the story using pictures and their memory of a story

- Begin to match spoken words with print

- May know some letter names and some letter sound associations

- May recognize some words and letters in their environment or in texts; but not again in a different context; they may still be unsure of the concept of "word" or "letter"

- Can write some letters, usually those in their own names

- In writing may reverse some letters, and may use mostly uppercase letters

- May make scribbles or strings of random letters with no spaces; one letter may represent a whole word

- May "read" or attribute meaning to his or her marks; may not be able to "re-read" these marks at a later time.

> It is much easier for a child to become an early reader if he has enjoyed being an emerging one and feels confident with his growing skills.

In summary, this description means that five-year-olds generally have a sense that written language conveys meaning, but their grasp of the elements of written language is still tentative. The child takes a playful approach to written language, pretending to write and read, and is able to recognize some words but without great consistency. Many cannot yet recognize or write all the letters of the alphabet with accuracy and consistency. Of great importance is that the child has a growing awareness of print literacy and feels comfortable with it. Like first becoming comfortable with water and then learning to swim, it is much easier for a child to become an early reader if he has enjoyed being an emerging one and feels confident with his growing skills.

Play-Based Versus Didactic Methods of Early Education

Long-term studies comparing the effects of play-based early education with those of didactic programs with intensive instruction are badly needed. The High/Scope Preschool Curriculum Comparison Study[19] is one of the few exemplary models. It followed preschool children until age 23. Similar research by Rebecca Marcon[20] followed preschool children until fourth grade. Both found that classrooms rich with child-initiated activity, including play, were considerably more effective for children from low-income backgrounds than didactic education.

Unfortunately, most of the research on this question looks at results only through kindergarten, first, or second grade. This is a grave flaw, because the High/Scope and Marcon studies strongly suggest that the benefits of play-based early education become visible only after several years. Most preschool and kindergarten interventions show some short-term gains in narrowly defined areas, but the real test is whether the gains hold up over time.

Positive short-term results may be misleading in another way. They tend to focus on the variables that are easiest to measure, like knowledge of the alphabet and decoding language skills. "Developing Early Literacy," a 2009 report by the National Early Literacy Panel (NELP), is a prime example.[21] NELP's mission was to identify early interventions that would lead to long-term literacy. Its meta-analysis of the studies that met its criteria focused on decoding and other discrete skills rather than on more complex measures that include rich language experiences.

A group of leading early childhood experts including David K. Dickinson and Susan B. Neuman responded to the NELP report as follows:

> We urge the public (curriculum developers, instructional designers, teachers, parents, and policymakers) to not only look at the code skills as they prepare preschool agendas, but to also heed the panel's finding on the importance of comprehensive language development, background knowledge and conceptual development in reading readiness and longer-term reading skill. Like the expert decoder who can sound-out the Hebrew or Greek letters without understanding the

> language and content [that] undergirds these skills, children in such a system might *mean to read* but never master *reading for meaning*.[22]

Kathleen Kennedy Manzo, in *Education Week*, summarized Dickinson's view that "vocabulary, oral language, and background knowledge may not demonstrate their value until 3rd or 4th grade when children need to comprehend more complex texts and information across subject areas."[23] In the same article, Neuman summed up her concerns about the report in this way: "The report is all about code, because code is what has been studied, but what we know is that code alone is not going to solve our educational problems."[24]

NELP looked at about 500 studies (having disqualified roughly 7,500 that did not meet its criteria) that examined a variety of discrete, measurable skills. It did not review the effects of providing a language-rich environment. Such environments are often full of child-initiated play and learning, but their effects are harder to measure than those of narrow skills-based approaches. The panel also eliminated all qualitative studies from consideration. Yet qualitative studies, such as the Sarah Lawrence research described in this report, often shed light on subtle but crucial aspects of education issues.

The NELP report did compare some play-based interventions with non-play ones. The panel examined 19 studies in this area. The report concludes "the comparison of studies in which the intervention was more fully seated in a play-based activity with studies in which the intervention was not particularly play-based did not result in significantly different outcomes."[25] In other words, the non-play interventions were not more

> **Most kindergarten interventions show short-term gains, but the real test is whether the gains hold up in fourth grade and beyond.**

effective than the play-based ones. Given the critical importance of play in children's development and its documented decline in children's lives, this conclusion should be taken as a strong endorsement of play-based activities in kindergarten.

Unfortunately, the NELP report is likely to promote even more of what young children are already getting: long hours in kindergarten and preschool of teacher-led instruction in literacy skills and testing—and a dearth of child-initiated learning.

Unrealistic Standards

The literacy standards for kindergartners in New York and California, where the research described in Chapter 2 took place, offer a mixed picture of adult expectations for kindergartners. Many of the standards fit the Bank Street guidelines for emerging literacy and, taken one at a time, seem reasonable. But the sheer number of standards and their specificity is daunting. No wonder teachers spend so much of their time trying to meet them.

At the same time, some of the standards are deeply puzzling. Who decided that kindergartners in California should be able to recognize and name all uppercase and lowercase letters of the alphabet[26] and write them "independently, attending to the form and proper spacing of the letters"?[27] Emergent readers often can name and identify only some letters, and reversing letters is still quite normal for them.

In Tennessee, where parents have complained that their kindergarten children are expected to read before entering first grade, one of the "accomplishments" listed in the state kindergarten standards is that children should "read as 'an emergent reader' a favorite story with fluent intonation and phrasing."[28] This language suggests a reading level associated with first- or second-graders, not kindergartners.

By placing these demands in kindergarten, schools force teachers to spend most of their time trying to meet them. Teachers who recognize the gap between where their children are developmentally and what is required of them are in a difficult spot.

> There is a long-established view that kindergartners are quite different developmentally from first-graders and that their education should reflect that difference.

For some children, unrealistic standards do no harm. There will always be children who become skilled readers and writers in preschool or kindergarten, but they are in the minority. Their early development should not set the standard for all children. Many kindergartners show little or no interest in reading but arrive at first grade ready and eager to begin mastering written language.

When policymakers and educators now speak of "school readiness" they mean readiness for kindergarten, not first grade. But the Bank Street College guidelines tell us that it is not until first grade that children generally move from being emergent readers to early readers. This fits with the long-established view of child development that recognizes a significant difference between kindergarten children and first-graders and how they learn.

For generations kindergarten was seen as a child's garden, where faithful gardeners supported children's healthy growth and prepared them for success in school and a lifelong love of learning. Americans who are obsessed with speed may see this as a hopelessly old-fashioned view of school. We refer them to a new coalition of distinguished educators and thinkers, including Linda Darling-Hammond, Deborah Meier, Diane Ravitch, Sharon Lynn Kagan, and Susan Neuman, who are working toward what they call "a broader, bolder approach" to education. They recently called for "every American child to arrive at the *starting line of first grade* [emphasis ours] ready and able to learn."[29]

Nurturing, playful kindergartens are not the solution to every learning problem. Some children at high risk of school failure need more direct attention to their problems. More research is needed on the most effective approaches and interventions to assure them of the success they are entitled to in school. But demanding that they meet unrealistic standards has only added to their problems.

Failing Kindergarten

The bar for kindergarten achievement has been raised so that it is essentially at the level of first-grade achievement 20 years ago. Some children glide over the new bar easily. But many strain to keep up and pay a price. Others simply cannot make it. They are the ones who fail kindergarten.

The current fashion is to rely heavily on retention in grade to address academic failure. A 2002 California report estimated that by ninth grade 30 to 50 percent of students have been retained at least once.[30] Retention has filtered down to kindergarten, which has seen a rapid increase in the practice. In Texas, for example, kindergarten retention rates rose by two and a half times from 1994 to 2004, the highest increase of all the elementary grades.[31] In North Carolina kindergarten retention doubled between 1992 and 2002.[32] (Suspension and expulsion of kindergartners are also on the rise; see Chapter 6 for a discussion of this issue.)

Retention raises several troubling issues. One is that it happens most often to certain populations. Children are more likely to be held back if they have moved often, have limited English skills, are minority males, or come from low-income backgrounds. They are also more likely to be

> Demanding that children at risk of failure meet developmentally inappropriate standards has added to their problems.

retained if they are small in stature, or if the parents are unwilling or unable to intercede for the child.[33]

The North Carolina Kindergarten Readiness Issues Group surveyed research about retention in kindergarten and the lower grades. It concluded:

> Retention in the early elementary grades, especially before second grade, is harmful. Students retained in first grade have been found to do worse academically and socially compared to other low-performing students who were not retained. Negative effects have also been found for kindergartners who were retained.[34]

The National Association of School Psychologists identified several outcomes associated with retention: "Most children do not 'catch up' when held back. Although some retained students do better at first, these children often fall behind again in later grades. Students who are held back tend to get into trouble, dislike school, and feel badly [sic] about themselves more often than children who go on to the next grade."[35] Being retained increases the likelihood of dropping out of school later. "Even more staggering is the fact that being held back twice makes dropping out of school a virtual certainty."[36]

The National Association for the Education of Young Children rejected retention as a viable option for young children in a 2001 position statement:

> Retention policies should be highly suspect given the lack of demonstrated effectiveness and prevalent bias against certain groups of children. The current methodology used in selecting students for retention makes it impossible to predict accurately who will benefit. Pro-retention policies as a strategy for establishing rigorous academic standards are likely to be self-defeating. Lowered expectations developed by parents and teachers actually decrease the probability that retained children will attain their potential.[37]

Sam Meisels, president of the Erikson Institute in Chicago and an expert on the assessment of young children, recommends that retention be used rarely, and that new approaches to curriculum development, school restructuring, and student instruction should become the focus of academic improvement.[38]

Long-term studies that look at the consequences of kindergarten retention at fourth grade and beyond are needed. Some studies show academic improvements for children who are held back, but these are usually in the first and second grades. Retained students often do better at first but then fall behind in later grades. The U.S. Early Childhood Longitudinal Study—Kindergarten Cohort, which followed a group of kindergartners from 1998 through the eighth grade, may yield more information on long-term outcomes than is currently available. One study using this data showed that reading gains among children retained in kindergarten had disappeared by third grade while math gains still were present.[39]

> **Retention in kindergarten has increased even though research indicates that it does not help children and can do serious harm.**

Building on Children's Strengths

There are alternatives to retention and so-called social promotion for children having difficulty in kindergarten. The first is to reform kindergarten standards so that they become developmentally appropriate guidelines for this age group. Then help teachers develop effective kindergarten programs rich in child-initiated play and playful learning, where most children can successfully learn and grow. There will still be children who need help to succeed in kindergarten, but there are many steps that can be taken, including one-on-one assistance in school and at-home programs with parents.

Often children who are at risk of school failure are viewed only through the lens of what they lack. Their strengths also need to be recognized. For instance, while children of low-income families frequently have a smaller vocabulary than children of more affluent families, research by the National Institutes of Health has shown that they have similar skills in areas such as verbal fluency, memory, and social abilities.[40]

Successful educators of children from low-income families like Deborah Meier, founder of the Central Park East schools in East Harlem and the Mission Hill School in Boston, often comment on how communicative low-income children are despite their lower levels of exposure to language and books. When educators build on what is strong and healthy in children as well as addressing deficits, children tend to respond with enthusiasm for learning.

Preschools and kindergartens designed primarily to address deficits look like factory farms or laboratories for force-feeding language into children. At the same time, children's ability to use language in their own creative play—an especially powerful motivator for learning and an important tool for language development—is seriously curtailed. It is not surprising that such force-feeding approaches are not yielding the long-term gains they promise.

CHAPTER 4

OUT-OF-CONTROL TESTING

MANY EDUCATION POLICYMAKERS IN THE U.S. have become convinced that the only way to improve public schools is through pervasive and continual measurement of children's knowledge using standardized tests, with rewards and punishments attached to the results. The people who design these policies don't use the words "rewards" or "punishments." Instead they use words like "accountability" and "incentives." But under this strict regime, in which test results count for almost everything, a more accurate description *is* "rewards and punishments."

This approach to solving the complex problems of public education comes straight out of business, marketing, and mass-production management manuals, which endlessly repeat some version of the mantra "what can't be measured can't be improved."[41]

New York City school officials, for example, announced in late 2007 that all kindergarten children in the city's public schools would be given a standardized I.Q. test to determine whether they qualified for "gifted and talented" classes.[42] A few months later they announced a plan to begin standardized testing of kindergarten, first-, and second-grade children as a way to evaluate schools' effectiveness. The test scores would become part of a formula, already in use, to assign letter grades—A to F—to all of the city's public schools. The scores and grades are then used to determine rewards and punishments, including cash bonuses for teachers and principals and whether principals will be fired and schools shut down. Before the new plan was announced, only test results from third grade up were counted.[43]

According to the *New York Times*, the school system's chief accountability officer, James S. Liebman, who developed the grading system, used the oft-repeated argument

> **The results of a standardized test at the kindergarten level have only a 50-50 chance of being accurate.**

that you wouldn't expect to treat someone who was sick without first taking the person's temperature.

But a standardized test is not a thermometer. Thermometers are generally very accurate and highly reliable. The results of a standardized test at the kindergarten level are as likely to be misleading as they are to be correct. (See below.)

In the same *New York Times* article, Lorrie Shepard, dean of the School of Education at the University of Colorado at Boulder, commented on New York City's testing plan:

> It sounds like a downward extension of whatever's good, but also what's bad about standardized testing in the higher grades, with more risk because we know that standardized testing isn't appropriate at those ages. Now

they're venturing into territory where many more people say that the negative will far outweigh any positive.[44]

Why have the people running our public schools become so committed to testing? Social critic Stephen Metcalf explains:

> For its most conservative enthusiasts, testing makes sense as a lone solution to school failure because, they insist, adequate resources are already in place, and only the threat of exposure and censure is necessary for schools to succeed. ... Liberal faddishness, not chronic underfunding of poorer schools or child poverty itself, is blamed for underachievement: "Child-centered" education, "progressive" education or "whole language"—each has been singled out as a social menace that can be vanquished only by applying a more rational, results-oriented and business-minded approach to public education.[45]

These results-oriented policies may work in the business arena (although recent events in the banking and finance industries cast serious doubt on that idea) and they certainly win votes for politicians. But do they work in public schools? Do they actually help children, particularly those from low-income families, as their proponents claim?

New York City's "Success": Reassessing the Numbers

New York City Mayor Michael Bloomberg and Schools Chancellor Joel Klein appeared before the U.S. House Committee on Education and Labor in July 2008 and presented their evidence that New York's testing and accountability policies had substantially closed the achievement gaps between white and minority children in math and reading at the fourth-grade and eighth-grade levels. The Mayor claimed that in some cases the gap was cut in half.[46]

But Jennifer Jennings of Columbia University and Sherman Dorn of the University of South Florida, writing in *Teachers College Record*, paint a different picture:

> Bloomberg and Klein's assertion was based on differences in the *proficiency rate*, or the percentages of students meeting the cut score that New York State defines as proficient. But proficiency is a misleading and inaccu-

rate way to measure achievement gaps, though political actors often prefer to employ this metric because it paints a more positive picture of progress than truly exists. ... [T]he problem is that we cannot differentiate between students who just made it over the proficiency bar and those who scored well above it. Proficiency rates can increase substantially by moving a small number of kids up a few points—just enough to clear the cut score—or by shifting the cut score itself down. But African American and Hispanic students may still lag far behind their white and Asian peers even as their proficiency rates increase.[47]

Another way to assess gains and losses in student learning is to look at New York's scores on the National Assessment of Educational Progress, tests that are given to fourth- and eighth-graders across the country. Jennings and Dorn report that when the National Center for Educational Statistics analyzed changes in New York scores relative to the gap between African American and white students or Hispanic and white students, they found no statistically significant changes between 2003 and 2007, the time period during which Bloomberg and Klein have run the city's public schools.[48]

Testing Young Children: Caution

Rigid testing policies do not make sense in early childhood education. Standardized testing of children under age eight, when used to make significant decisions about the child's education, is in direct conflict with the professional standards of every educational testing organization.

Why has there been no general outcry against these practices from educators? Some of them are unaware of the professional standards on testing young children. (One-third of the Los Angeles kindergarten teachers in the study described in Chapter 2 of this report had not taken even one course in early childhood education or child development.) Those who are aware of the standards are reluctant to speak out because they are literally afraid of losing their jobs.

The National Association for the Education of Young Children (NAEYC) cautioned against most forms of testing before the age of eight as early as 1987. The NAEYC recommended that children's progress be judged by the use

Kindergarten teachers in New York and Los Angeles said they spend 20–30 minutes per day preparing children for or giving them tests.

of developmentally appropriate practices such as informal assessments, including teacher observations and work assessments or portfolios, and not by standardized tests.[49]

The most recent revision (2000) of the position statement on testing developed by the National Association of Early Childhood Specialists in State Departments of Education and adopted by the NAEYC states:

> A major problem with kindergarten tests is that relatively few meet acceptable standards of reliability and validity. Based on several widely used tests, the probability of a child being misplaced is fifty percent—the same odds as flipping a coin. The burden of proof is on educational and testing professions to justify the decisions they make in the selection or creation of screening instruments. Otherwise, educators are left speculating about what the results mean. Flawed results lead to flawed decisions, wasted tax dollars, and misdiagnosed children.[50]

Some policymakers argue that standardized tests are preferable to assessments that require teacher observations or a review of students' work because the latter methods take too much time. But the evidence from New York and Los Angeles that kindergarten teachers spend 20 to 30 minutes per day preparing children for tests or giving the tests (cited in Chapter 2 of this report) suggests that they may in fact be devoting more time to testing than are teachers using observational or work-sampling assessments. These data, combined with the widely held view that standardized testing of children under age eight lacks validity and is unreliable, argue against standardized testing and in favor of other methods of assessment in kindergarten.

Kindergarten teachers in Clark County, Nevada have become so concerned about the amount of time they

must spend testing children that they have organized an advocacy group, United Kindergarten Teachers of Las Vegas, to try to influence education policymakers. The goals of the group, according to its web site, "are to reduce the number of instructional days lost to assessment, reduce class size, and have a return to the implementation of developmentally appropriate standards."[51]

The National Association of School Psychologists issued a position paper on early childhood assessment in 2005, stating that "evidence from research and practice in early childhood assessment indicates that issues of technical adequacy are more difficult to address with young children who have little test-taking experience, short attention spans, and whose development is rapid and variable."[52]

The Association for Childhood Education International went even further, stating "unequivocally the belief that *all* testing of young children in preschool and grades K–2 ... should cease."[53] It noted that standardized testing in the early years causes stress, does not provide useful information, leads to harmful tracking and labeling of children, causes teaching to the test, and fails to set conditions for cooperative learning and problem-solving.[54]

High Stakes and Inappropriate Expectations

In the late 1990s, responding to growing concerns about the negative effects of testing on children, Congress charged the National Research Council (NRC) with the task of studying the appropriate and inappropriate uses of standardized tests. The study committee's exhaustive report, published in 1999 with the title *High Stakes*, included the following statements regarding the testing of young children:

> Problems of test validity are greatest among young children, and there is a greater risk of error when such tests are employed to make significant educational decisions about children who are less than 8 years old or below grade 3—or about their schools. However, well-designed assessments may be useful in monitoring trends in the educational development of populations of students who have reached age 5.[55]

> Recommendation: In general, large-scale assessments should not be used to make high-stakes decisions

about students who are less than 8 years old or enrolled below grade 3.[56]

Anyone who has participated in the administration of standardized tests to five-year-olds understands the wisdom of this conclusion. Many kindergarten-age children are simply not mature enough to concentrate on the process of understanding and answering scripted questions within the time limits set by these assessments. They are even more affected than older children by the sense of portentous consequences that such testing entails. The same child may score well on a particular test on one day and fail the same test miserably the next day because of illness, apprehension, unexpected events, or out-of-school conditions that the test administrator is unaware of.

It is particularly unacceptable for standardized tests to be used as the primary source of information in making decisions about placing children in special education programs. Labeling children as learning disabled or hyperactive, for instance, requires complex methods of assessment. Symptoms of these conditions can in many cases be caused by inappropriate expectations of children who are being pushed to succeed at tasks they are developmentally unprepared for (see Chapter 3). We must always ask this question: To what extent is this child responding to an inappropriate form of education?

A new report from the NRC, issued in August 2008, specifically addresses the use of assessments with young children from birth to age five. It urges "extreme caution" in basing high-stakes decisions, like cutting funding for programs or determining that a child has a disability, on assessments of young children:

> Following the best possible assessment practices is especially crucial in cases in which assessment can have significant consequences for children, teachers, or programs. The 1999 NRC report *High Stakes: Testing for Tracking, Promotion, and Graduation* urged extreme caution in basing high-stakes decisions on assessment outcomes, and we conclude that even more extreme caution is needed when dealing with young children from birth to age 5 and with the early care and education system. We emphasize that a primary purpose of assessing children or classrooms is to improve the

quality of early childhood care and education by identifying where more support, professional development, or funding is needed and by providing classroom personnel with tools to track children's growth and adjust instruction.[57]

The report also concludes that the No Child Left Behind model of testing literacy and math skills, or any other explicitly defined academic content, is inappropriate in early education, because "well-defined academic content areas are not characteristic of excellent care and education for younger children."[58]

Further, the report states that negative consequences for children, teachers, or schools based on assessments of children should happen only if the teachers have received adequate support, professional development, and resources to meet expectations, and if the level of children's development when they entered the program has been taken into account. Child assessment results should never be the only information considered. And a program should not be closed or restructured if doing so would have "worse consequences for children than leaving it open," the report adds.[59]

The Alliance for Childhood believes that the conclusions of the 2008 NRC report apply to kindergarten children, teachers, and programs to the exact same degree that they apply in preschool. The committee, chaired by Professor Catherine Snow of Harvard, warned that some assessments commonly used by schools have been tested only with populations that are not representative of the diverse backgrounds, experiences, and needs of children in today's early childhood programs. In particular, many existing tests have not demonstrated their validity for assessing young children with special needs and those for whom English is a second language.[60] This caution applies to the tests being used in kindergarten as well.

Finally, the NRC committee wrote, programs should be evaluated not only on how they affect academic skills but also on whether they improve other important aspects of children's development, such as social and emotional skills. Tools for assessing other abilities such as problem-solving and creativity remain underdeveloped.[61]

Chapter 5

The Scripted Kindergarten: What the Research Tells Us

By its very nature, authentic child-initiated play does not follow a script. It is spontaneous and ever-changing. Thus it is especially important to take note of the increasing amount of scripted teaching that is taking place in U.S. kindergartens.

In scripted classrooms teachers must follow a highly regimented and invariable routine—literally, a script—in which prescribed activities and words are used and others are prohibited. The lessons are linked to standardized tests given at frequent intervals to measure children's progress in learning the approved facts and skills.

Advocates of scripted teaching argue that systemic change, especially in urban schools, won't happen unless teachers know exactly what is expected of them. Eric Smith, former superintendent of the Charlotte-Mecklenburg school district in North Carolina and a proponent of scripted curricula, says that, because of the diversity of experience among teachers, it is "the job of the superintendent of schools to bring that kind of clarity to the classroom and give the teachers the strategies that will help them to be successful."[62]

Critics of scripted teaching argue that it undermines teacher-student relationships and is based on a simplistic and flawed model of how young children learn. Lawrence Schweinhart and the late David Weikart of the High/Scope Educational Research Foundation, in a critique of Direct Instruction, an early scripted curriculum, wrote: "Direct Instruction ... seeks to transfer information rather than encourage problem-solving, discovery, or curiosity. Adults are authorities who tell children what to do and what to think, rather than guides who assist children in puzzling through situations and deciding for themselves what they should do."[63]

What does scripted teaching actually look like? One teacher described it this way:

> Imagine walking down the halls of your school and hearing the same sentences read, the same questions asked, and the same teacher comments coming from each classroom. "Impossible," you say to yourself. "This could not possibly be happening." But it is. This scenario is becoming more and more commonplace throughout schools in the United States as scripted curriculum materials are implemented more widely.[64]

Given how prevalent scripted curricula have become in kindergartens[65] and elementary classrooms—and even in preschools—it is remarkable how uninformed Americans are about their existence. This is probably because they are used primarily in schools serving large numbers of children from low-income families. It is hard to imagine

> In scripted classrooms teachers must follow a highly regimented and invariable routine in which some activities and words are required and others are prohibited.

more affluent parents accepting such an approach for their children.

The modern trend toward scripted education began with Siegfried Engelmann and Carl Bereiter in the 1960s. Their program, originally called DISTAR (Direct Instruction System for Teaching Arithmetic and Reading) and later renamed Direct Instruction, was one of three approaches studied by the High/Scope Educational Research Foundation in its important Preschool Curriculum Comparison Study.

The study randomly assigned 68 at-risk children from low-income homes to one of three programs. DISTAR was used in one classroom; the other two were a traditional nursery school and a High/Scope preschool, both with a strong emphasis on child-initiated activity. At first, the three approaches seemed equally sound. Children's I.Q. scores in all three groups rose by 27 points, and other gains were also documented.

But after a year or two, significant differences began to appear. By age 15 the youngsters who had attended the DISTAR program self-reported twice as many delinquent acts as those in the other two groups. They also reported "relatively poor relations with their families, less participation in sports, fewer school job appointments, and less reaching out to others for help with personal problems."[66] The follow-up continued until the subjects were 23 years old. The researchers concluded:

> Findings at age 23 continue to support the conclusion that the High/Scope and Nursery School groups are better off than the Direct Instruction group in a variety of ways. Either the High/Scope group, the Nursery School group, or both, show statistically significant advantages over the Direct Instruction group on 17 variables. Most important, compared with the Direct Instruction Group, the High/Scope and Nursery School groups have had significantly fewer felony arrests of various kinds and fewer years of special education for emotional impairment. In addition, compared with the Direct Instruction group, the High/Scope group aspires to complete a higher level of schooling, and has more members living with their spouses. It thus appears that preschool programs that promote child-initiated activities (such as the High/Scope and Nursery School programs) seem to

In scripted teaching, "adults are authorities who tell children what to do and what to think, rather than guides who assist children in puzzling through situations and deciding for themselves what they should do."

—LAWRENCE SCHWEINHART & DAVID WEIKART

contribute to the development of an individual's sense of personal and social responsibility.[67]

During the 1970s and '80s the scripted method lost ground in favor of child-initiated learning, but as didactic instruction became more popular during the 1990s, educators again looked toward scripted teaching. It *seemed* to be more effective than other didactic approaches. But there is little valid research to support this view. The Promising Practices Network (PPN), a division of RAND Corporation, assesses research on educational practices. It found that nearly 100 studies of Direct Instruction had been done since the 1960s; all but 20 of them failed to meet PPN standards for methodological rigor. Of these 20, only four showed positive effects of Direct Instruction compared to other programs; eight showed mixed results, and four found no significant results.[68]

Margaret Moustafa and Robert Land of California State University in Los Angeles conducted a large-scale study of southern California schools serving a majority of children from low-income families. They looked at the test results of nearly 100,000 children in 183 schools that used scripted curricula (either Open Court or Success for All) and compared them with test results from schools using non-scripted curricula between 1999 and 2001.

They pointed out that their results need to be understood in the broader context of interpreting high-stakes standardized test scores. Many researchers have noted that after a new test is introduced scores at first fall and then tend to rise steadily from year to year. Thus California schools saw a steady rise in scores on the Stanford Achievement Test (SAT 9) during the years in which it was given. Within this rising pattern, Moustafa and Land found that the percentage of children scoring at or above the 50th percentile was (1) lower in schools with scripted programs than in schools with unscripted programs; (2) lower in schools with fewer credentialed teachers than in schools with more credentialed teachers; and (3) lowest in schools with fewer credentialed teachers *and* with scripted programs.[69]

> Students who went to playful preschools had significantly fewer felony arrests and fewer years of special education for emotional impairment than similar students who went to a didactic, scripted-teaching preschool.

In a separate analysis of the Open Court Reading program (which is used by the great majority of the Los Angeles kindergarten teachers who participated in the U.C.L.A. study reported in Chapter 2 of this report) the researchers summarized their findings as follows:

Altogether, the outcomes in the Alief, Inglewood, and Los Angeles school districts suggest that *Open Court* limits what children are able to achieve in literacy relative to what they are able to achieve via many other programs. The outcomes support the professional judgment of the reading/language arts teacher specialists on California's 1996 Instructional Resources Evaluation Panel who recommended *Open Court* not be placed on California's textbook adoption list. Finally, we find no justification in sacrificing instruction in other core curricular areas to implement *Open Court.*[70]

The case for scripted teaching suffered further blows when the Department of Education's own Institute of Education Sciences (IES) reviewed 30 studies of Open Court Reading that were published or released between 1985 and 2007. It found that none of the studies met its evidence standards and therefore could not be used to draw conclusions about the effectiveness of the program.[71]

A separate study by IES of Reading First, a federal program that committed $6 billion over six years to ensure that schools serving low-income families would use literacy programs in kindergarten through grade three that were proven successful, found that its programs, including Open Court, did not yield gains on the most important of Reading First's five goals: comprehension of written material.[72] While decoding skills did increase in the early grades, comprehension did not. Decoding skills are easier to teach and measure than more important aspects of literacy such as comprehension.

Education Week summarized the IES findings this way: "While more time is spent on reading instruction and professional development in schools that received Reading First grants than in comparison schools, students in participating schools are no more likely to become proficient readers, even after several years with the extended instruction, the study found."[73]

An earlier report by the government's General Accountability Office had revealed corrupt practices in the committee that decided which curricula should be funded under Reading First. It found that at least three committee members received royalties or profits from curricula they helped develop and then chose for the list of approved programs.[74] With the federal government giving out a billion dollars a year for such programs, the stakes are indeed high.

> Scripted teaching is a vast experiment with virtually no basis in valid research.

CHAPTER 6

PLAY AND CHILDREN'S HEALTH: A VITAL CONNECTION

PLAY IS ONE OF THE VITAL SIGNS of health in children.[75] Parents intuitively recognize this and often describe the severity of a child's illness by how much he is able to play. When a child is very ill, play ceases. It returns when the child is well again.

If play is such a strong indicator of children's well-being, what happens when children grow up without adequate opportunities for play? How does this affect their immediate and long-term health, both physical and mental?

The American Academy of Pediatrics expressed concern about the demise of play in a clinical report issued in October 2006. Its recommendations included the following:

Pediatricians can promote free play as a healthy, essential part of childhood. They should recommend that all children are afforded ample, unscheduled, independent, nonscreen time to be creative, to reflect, and to decompress. They should emphasize that although parents can certainly monitor play for safety, a large proportion of play should be child-driven rather than adult-directed.

Pediatricians should emphasize the advantages of active play and discourage parents from the overuse of passive entertainment (e.g., television and computer games).

Pediatricians should emphasize that active child-centered play is a time-tested way of producing healthy, fit young bodies.[76]

Parents and other professionals who work with children should be in partnership with doctors in advocating for play. The United States can learn from the United Kingdom, where play is taken seriously and where the profession of playwork is well established. Thousands of highly skilled U.K. playworkers work with children of all ages and all abilities in a wide range of settings: adven-

ture playgrounds, parks, schools, and other places where children gather and play.[77] With organizations such as Play England and Play Wales, playworkers advocate for play and advise their governments—which have national policies for play.

> Many health professionals see a link between the decline in active outdoor play and the rise in childhood obesity.

Nonetheless, play is threatened in the U.K.—as it is in the U.S.—for a variety of reasons. In 2006 the London *Telegraph* published an open letter signed by 110 educators, health professionals, and childhood advocates worried about a marked decline in children's health. "We are deeply concerned at the escalating incidence of childhood depression and children's behavioral and developmental conditions," they wrote.[78] A follow-up letter in 2007, signed by nearly 300 educators, authors, and advocates, focused on the need for more play to reverse the deterioration of children's well-being: "We believe that a key factor in this disturbing trend is the marked decline over the last 15 years in children's play." It added, "Real play—socially interactive, firsthand, loosely supervised—has always been a vital part of children's development, and its loss could have serious implications."

What are some of those implications? Many health professionals see a link between the decline in active outdoor play and the rise in childhood obesity. A typical school-aged child today spends four to six hours with high-tech media, most of it indoors,[79] and less than one hour outdoors in non-sports activities.[80]

Research on the link between declining play and obesity is badly needed, but one study sheds light on the issue. The *Harvard Heart Letter* published data on the number of calories burned by adults of different weights in a wide range of physical activities. An adult weighing 125 pounds playing children's games like hopscotch or jacks, for example, burns 150 calories in 30 minutes. This is less than running or bicycling but considerably more than sitting in front of a screen, which burns only 23 calories in the same amount of time.[81]

It is thus not surprising that childhood obesity is on the rise. Because of obesity-related problems such as high blood pressure and diabetes, doctors now warn that today's children may be the first generation in 200 years to have a shorter lifespan than their parents.[82]

Another area of concern is the rise in mental illness among children. Again, we know of no solid research linking the demise of play with this increase, but given the many ways that play strengthens the social and emotional life of children and relieves stress, it is likely that its decline contributes to mental problems.

The overall picture of children's mental health is summarized by psychologist Sharna Olfman in this way:

> The number of American children being diagnosed with psychiatric illnesses has soared over the past decade and a half. The National Institute of Mental Health (NIMH) estimates that today one in ten children and adolescents in the United States "suffers from mental illness severe enough to result in significant functional impairment." During this same time period, psychotropic drugs have become the treatment of first choice rather than the treatment of last resort. Recent years have witnessed a threefold increase in the use of psychotropic medications among patients under twenty years of age, and prescriptions for preschoolers have been skyrocketing. Over 10 million children and adolescents are currently on antidepressants, and about 5 million children are taking stimulant medications such as Ritalin.[83]

A 2009 study by University of Missouri researchers tracked first-grade girls until seventh grade. They found links between students' weak academic performance in the first grade, self-perception in the sixth grade, and depression symptoms in the seventh grade:

> "We found that students in the first grade who struggled academically with core subjects, including reading and math, later displayed negative self-perceptions and symptoms of depression in sixth and seventh grade, respectively," said Keith Herman, associate professor of education. …"Often, children with poor academic skills believe they have less influence on important outcomes in their life. Poor academic skills can influence how children view themselves as students and as social beings."[84]

The researchers advise that the curriculum be broadened so that children who excel in nonacademic areas also have a chance to show their skills in interpersonal relations, athletics, and music. We would add play to that list. Children of all ages, but especially younger ones, need a broad-based curriculum that includes play, recess, the arts, and a wide range of activities that allow the full scope of a child's capacities to blossom.

> Kindergarten aggression came to wide public attention in 2007 when an elementary school in Florida called the police to arrest a kindergartner for throwing a flailing, kicking tantrum.

If one in ten children suffers from mental illness, then in a typical classroom we can expect two or three children to be suffering in this way, often untreated. We need to be especially careful about adding stress to their lives. Some stress cannot be avoided, but stress related to inappropriate educational goals can be avoided.

Romper Room to Raging Kindergartners

We believe that current kindergarten conditions are contributing to high levels of frustration, stress, and even aggression in kindergartners. Research on these problems is badly needed, but a growing number of studies and anecdotal reports point to a clear increase in serious behavioral problems among kindergartners. Many experts see a probable link between extreme behaviors and the pressures of testing and unreasonable expectations.

Kindergarten aggression came to wide public attention in 2007 when an elementary school in Florida called the police to arrest a kindergartner for throwing a flailing, kicking tantrum. She was handcuffed, charged with a felony (battery on a school official), fingerprinted, and taken to jail. When Bob Herbert of the *New York Times* said to the police chief, "But she was six," the chief replied, "Do you think this is the first six-year-old we've arrested?"[85]

Most school administrators find alternatives to calling the police when a young child becomes violent. But the problem of kindergarten rage is getting worse. The *Hartford Courant* reported that Connecticut students in the earliest grades, including kindergarten, are increasingly behaving in ways that pose physical threats to themselves and others.[86] Connecticut schools suspended or expelled 901 kindergartners for fighting, defiance, or temper tantrums in 2002; this was almost twice as many as in 2000.[87]

One New Haven school official attributed the spike in violence among young children to the increasing emphasis on standardized testing and the elimination of time for recess, gym, and other chances to play. "It's not like it was when we were kids, when you could expect to have an hour or so every day to play and explore," she said. "That kind of time just isn't there anymore."[88]

The Mayor's Commission for Children in Springfield, Missouri responded to reports of increased aggression in kindergarten classrooms by studying the situation in some depth. In 2005 the commission sent questionnaires to all kindergarten teachers and elementary school principals in Springfield and neighboring Republic, Missouri, a total of 146 educators. Nearly 96 percent responded. Of these, about 75 percent said that they were seeing increases in aggression in their classrooms. Teachers reported that an average of 15 percent of their time was spent managing aggressive behavior in the classroom.[89]

A *Time* magazine article in 2003 linked aggressive behaviors with rising academic pressure in kindergarten and first grade in anticipation of the yearly tests demanded by the No Child Left Behind Act. Stephen Hinshaw, a professor of psychology at the University of California, Berkeley and an expert in hyperactive disorders, spoke of the need for a broad-based kindergarten approach: "Even more vital than early reading is the learning of play skills, which form the foundation of cognitive skills," he said. He pointed out that in Europe children are often not taught to read until age seven. "Insisting that they read at 5," he said, "puts undue pressure on a child."[90]

Psychiatrist Bruce Perry, an expert on childhood trauma and stress, sees a downward trend in children's overall emotional health. Children who are chronologically six years old are showing up in school with the "emotional experience you would expect of a three-year-old," he told

> Too many schools place a double burden on young children. First, they heighten their stress by demanding that they master material beyond their developmental level. Then they deprive children of their chief means of dealing with that stress—creative play.

Time's Claudia Wallis. "Imagine a child with the terrible twos in a six-year-old body. It's a huge problem in education and mental-health circles."[91]

Given the high rates of mental illness and/or aggressive behavior among young children today, it is critically important that early education practices promote physical and emotional health and not exacerbate illness. But too many schools today are placing a double burden on young children: First, they heighten their stress levels by demanding that they master material that is often beyond their developmental level. Then they deprive children of their chief means of dealing with that stress—creative play.

Addressing Kindergarten Aggression

Aggression and other behavioral difficulties are also showing up in preschool classrooms. Dr. Walter Gilliam of Yale University surveyed preschools in 40 states and found expulsion rates were three times higher than national rates for grades K–12. In addition, he found that 4.5 times as many boys as girls were being expelled.[92]

Journalist Peg Tyre, author of the book *The Trouble with Boys*, summarizes the research on the problems young boys face in schools:

> The way we educate our children and the messages they get from the community have changed a great deal in the last 15 years. I've come to believe from my research ... that many of these changes—although well-intentioned—have been bad for boys. Little children get less and less unstructured free time. In school, we've had an acceleration of academics, a narrowing of the curriculum and, in an effort to boost test scores, many schools have a schedule that isn't in line with what is developmentally appropriate for lots of children, especially boys. In our post-Columbine world, there is also less tolerance for boy behavior. Anti-violence policies, which are good, have evolved into anti-fantasy-violence policies, which I think deny boys (who, for better or worse, think and play a lot around violence) a chance to be their authentic selves in school.[93]

What happens to young children who display serious behavioral problems in preschools and kindergartens? In Texas they are sent to special schools for children with

Preschool expulsion rates are three times higher than national rates for grades K–12, and boys are being expelled 4–5 times more often than girls.

severe disciplinary problems, and may remain there for many years. Texas Appleseed, a public interest law center, reported in 2007 that over a five-year period "110 school districts in Texas have referred pre-k and kindergarten children to Disciplinary Alternative Education Programs (DAEPs), despite a statutory ban on placement of children under the age of 6 into these programs unless they have brought a firearm to school."[94]

Texas Appleseed studied the pathway from school to prison and found that placement in a DAEP considerably increased a youngster's likelihood of later going to prison. It would seem absurd to talk about prison and kindergarten in the same breath were it not for two things: First, the High/Scope Educational Research Foundation found years ago that low-income children who attended a scripted preschool program later had higher incarceration rates than those attending programs with more play and hands-on experiential learning.[95]

Second, some states now predict the number of prison cells they will need by looking at the number of children who fail the third-grade reading tests—so closely aligned is failure to learn to read linked with incarceration. The latter fact makes many push for higher reading standards at younger ages. But, again, there is no research evidence that moving first-grade reading expectations into kindergarten has any long-term positive effect on comprehension or developing a love of reading. Play and playful learning in rich early education environments that include oral and print literacy and are supported by good teachers offer a much greater likelihood of success. See the discussion of research on this issue in Chapter 1, including the summary of findings in *A Mandate for Playful Learning in Preschool*.[96]

Some states now predict the number of prison cells they will need by looking at the number of children who fail the third-grade reading tests.

A Call to Action on the Education of Young Children issued by the Alliance for Childhood in 2005 expressed serious concern about the ways early childhood education was contributing to pressure and stress in children's lives. The statement was signed by Howard Gardner, Daniel Goleman, Jane Goodall, David Elkind, Linda Darling-Hammond, and hundreds of others. It reads, in part:

> ... current trends in early education policy and practice heighten pressure and stress in children's lives, which can contribute to behavioral and learning problems.

We call for research on the causes of increased levels of anger, misbehavior, and school expulsion among young children.[97]

One way researchers gauge anxiety in children is to measure how sweaty the children's palms are. In one study of anxious children, those who were allowed to engage in make-believe play showed lower stress levels than those who were not allowed to play.[98] This clinical finding confirms what most observant parents and teachers of young children have known for a long time—that it is through open-ended play that children work through and make sense of scary, confusing, and frustrating experiences.

In medicine a guiding principle is "First, do no harm." The same should apply in education. Current early childhood practices are almost certainly doing harm to many children. These practices must be changed. The beauty of good education is that, like good medicine, it can promote healing. A healthy education addresses the full range of a child's needs—physical, social, emotional, and cognitive—and can help to restore balance to a child's life.

CHAPTER 7

CREATING THE PLAYFUL KINDERGARTEN:
IDEAS FOR EDUCATORS AND POLICYMAKERS

IN GENERAL, CHILD-INITIATED PLAY HAS FALLEN OUT OF FAVOR as a foundation for learning in kindergarten. Yet the evidence supporting its central role is abundant. Teachers and administrators must understand what play offers young children and be able to speak clearly about it. Parents also need to be well informed. "Play has to be reframed and seen not as an opposite to work but rather as a complement," says psychologist David Elkind. "Curiosity, imagination, and creativity are like muscles: if you don't use them, you lose them."[99]

Vivian Gussin Paley, the MacArthur Award–winning author of numerous books in which children's voices at play are beautifully captured, recommends keeping daily journals of what children say and do during their play. These observations can help convince others of the value of play—and of the time required for it to flower:

> We continue to call play the work of young children while reducing its appearance to brief interludes. There is barely time to develop a plot or transform a bad guy into a hero. The educational establishment has ceased admiring the stunning originality of its youngest students, preferring lists of numerical and alphabetical achievement goals.[100] ... Having not listened carefully enough to their play, we did not realize how much time was needed by children in order to create the scenery and develop the skills for their ever-changing dramas. We removed the element—time—that enabled play to be effective, then blamed the children when their play skills did not meet our expectations.[101]

Elena Bodrova and Deborah Leong, early childhood researchers who developed the "Tools of the Mind" curriculum, summarize the abundant research documenting the benefits of play and the developmental gains associated with it:

Play has been of great interest to scholars of child development and learning, psychologists, and educators alike. Jean Piaget (1962) and Lev Vygotsky (1978) were among the first to link play with cognitive development. In a comprehensive review of numerous studies on play, researchers found evidence that play contributes to advances in "verbalization, vocabulary, language comprehension, attention span, imagination, concentration, impulse control, curiosity, problem-solving strategies, cooperation, empathy, and group participation."[102] ... Further, research directly links play to children's ability to master such academic content as literacy and numeracy. For example, children's engagement in pretend play was found to be positively and significantly correlated with such competencies as text comprehension and

Research directly links play to children's ability to master such academic content as literacy and numeracy.

metalinguistic awareness and with an understanding of the purpose of reading and writing.[103]

Integrating Child-Directed Play and Focused Learning Through Play

The playful kindergarten relies on child-initiated play with the active presence of a teacher, combined with intentional teaching through playful learning, the arts, and other hands-on experiences. The line between child-initiated play and engagement with playful teacher-led activity is sometimes distinct and sometimes thin and porous. The two can reinforce each other, such as when teachers present stories and other activities that inspire the playful imagination. In contrast, the more didactic instruction becomes, the more detached it tends to be from the child's deep-rooted ways of learning.

The authors of *A Mandate for Playful Learning in Preschool* summarize their review of the research as follows:

[B]oth free play and playful learning should command a central role in high-quality education for preschoolers. (Italics theirs.) Children taught in a more playful manner almost always achieve more than children who are subjected to more direct teaching methods. Further-

more, the data show that academic programs that emphasize more direct instruction have unintended social and emotional consequences, creating students who are less likely to get along with their peers and feel comfortable in school, and more likely to show evidence of stress-induced hyperactivity, to be hostile, and to engage in antisocial acts.[104]

Professor Diane Levin of Wheelock College in Boston has spent 35 years researching and teaching about the ways young children learn through play. She sees a dynamic interaction between teacher and child at the heart of learning, and she describes a matrix of early childhood classrooms using the variables of the teacher's input and the children's initiative (see diagram below). This interaction is especially important in today's media-saturated world, says Levin, where many children have not learned how to engage in rich play of their own making and need a teacher's help creating it.

Early education based on large amounts of didactic instruction—and especially scripted teaching—involves high levels of teacher input but little initiative from children. At the other extreme, in the laissez-faire classroom, the children are very active, often in an unfocused way,

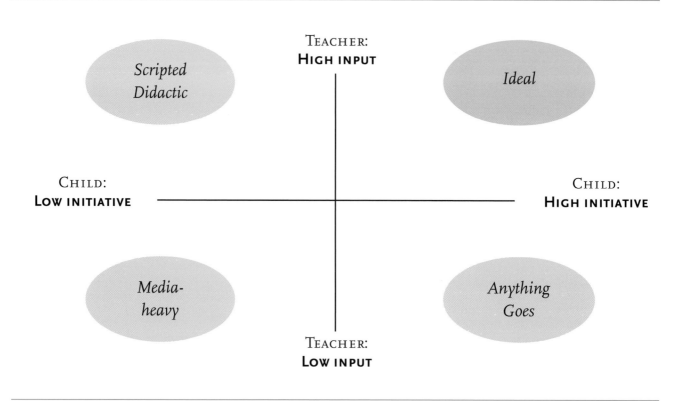

> The dynamic interaction between teacher and child is especially important in today's media-saturated world, where many children have not learned how to engage in rich play of their own making and need a teacher's help creating it.

and the teachers are largely passive. In classrooms that rely heavily on electronic media both teachers and children have low levels of activity. Levin says that in the ideal classroom children are engaged, taking initiative to the extent they are able, and teachers are also active in building on children's play (without taking control of it) as they engage children with intentional but playful activities.

In playful kindergartens teachers are active in many different ways. They closely observe children's play and take cues from it, enriching and enlarging its scope by bringing new materials into the environment. A teacher might develop a theme from the children's make-believe scenarios that will extend their knowledge through artistic and experiential activities. Teachers in playful kindergartens focus on the development of strong relationships with their students, and on the healthy development of each individual child.

Kindergarten teachers should know the typical stages of development of five-year-olds. They need to encourage all facets of that development, and they should recognize when and how to intervene if the child's growth is seriously atypical or there are signs of a disability. The play-based approach calls for teachers to know each child well and to differentiate their teaching methods to meet individual needs. It is the antithesis of the one-size-fits-all model of education.

Making Room for All Types of Play

Play has many faces. Climbing a tree is different from building a house with sticks and stones or dressing up for make-believe play. Yet when the child is up in the tree she may well become a pirate surveying the sea around her. There are different types of play, but they often overlap in rich play scenarios. The well-developed player has a repertoire with many forms of play; the playful kindergarten supports them all.

Play does not stay neatly in categories, but knowing and watching for the broad types helps sensitize teachers and parents to the shifting landscapes children create. It also provides a tool for assessing whether a playful kindergarten is providing adequate opportunity and materials for all types of play. Twelve key types of play are:

Large-motor play: Children love to climb, run, slide, swing, jump, and engage in every type of movement possible. Such play develops coordination, balance, and a sense of one's body in the space around it.

Small-motor play: Play with small toys and activities like stringing beads, playing with puzzles, and sorting objects into types develops dexterity.

Mastery play: Children often repeat an action in play and persevere until they master it, such as making dozens of "birthday packages" to learn to tie bows, or playing on a balance beam to become a "circus performer."

Rules-based play: Kindergartners and grade-school children enjoy the challenge of making up their own rules and the social negotiation involved in adapting the rules for each play situation.

Construction play: Building houses, ships, forts, and other structures is a basic form of play that requires skill and imagination.

Make-believe play: This broad category incorporates many other play types and is rich with language, problem-solving, and imagination. It frequently begins with "Let's pretend" and goes on to include anything children might have experienced or imagined.

Symbolic play: Children take an object at hand and convert it into the toy or prop they need through a fluid process of fantasy or imagination.

Language play: Children develop mastery by playing with words, rhymes, verses, and songs they make up or change. They tell stories and dramatize them. They are fascinated by foreign languages, especially when they are presented playfully in story, verse, or song.

Playing with the arts: Children integrate all forms of art into their play, using whatever materials are at hand to draw, model, create music, perform puppet shows, and so on. They explore the arts and use them to express their feelings and ideas.

Sensory play: Most children enjoy playing with dirt, sand, mud, water, and other materials with different textures, sounds, and smells. Such play develops the senses.

Rough-and-tumble play: This fundamental form of play is found in animals as well as human children. Animals know how to play roughly without injury by rounding their body gestures and not aiming for dominance. Children can be helped to do the same if their play becomes too aggressive.

Risk-taking play: Children extend their abilities through risky play and learn to master challenging environments. They generally know how far they can go without actually hurting themselves. Regrettably, most current play spaces are designed to be as risk-free as possible, giving children little chance to assess risks and set their own boundaries.

Educating Teachers for Play

Educating kindergarten teachers so that they can develop strong and effective play-based programs will be a challenge, requiring workshops, courses, and mentoring as well as educational materials in the form of print, film, webinars, web sites, and other media. Teacher-education programs and teachers experienced in play-based kindergartens will be called upon to educate and support classroom teachers.

One challenge in educating teachers for playful kindergartens is that many younger teachers did not grow up with a strong experience of child-initiated play. Their free time was filled with electronic media and organized activities. They will need to experience play themselves to understand its powerful nature and its role in effective kindergarten education. The same can be said of younger parents. A major task will be to help parents and educators recapture the spirit of play.

Bonnie Neugebauer of Child Care Information Exchange has written about adults who live with the spirit of play and the vital role they play for children. She describes them this way:

> They play with words and ideas. They use toys, invent props, appropriate resources for new purposes. They play with children and with other adults. They play because it is natural and because it makes them feel good. Children need these adults in their lives, people who will model the importance of play to living. But in so many early childhood programs, people have forgotten how to be playful. They are focused on order and routines, appearances and paperwork, agendas and lesson plans. There is no serendipity, no wonder, no surprise.[105]

> "Children need [playful] adults in their lives, people who will model the importance of play to living."
>
> —BONNIE NEUGEBAUER

TWELVE KEY TYPES OF PLAY

THERE ARE DIFFERENT TYPES OF PLAY, and they often overlap in rich play scenarios. Knowing and watching for the broad types helps sensitize teachers and parents to the shifting landscapes children create. It also provides a tool for assessing whether a playful kindergarten is providing adequate opportunity and materials for all types of play.

Large-motor play

Children love to climb, run, slide, swing, jump, and engage in every type of movement possible. Such play develops coordination, balance, and a sense of one's body in the space around it.

Small-motor play

Play with small toys and activities like stringing beads, playing with puzzles, and sorting objects into types develops dexterity.

Mastery play

Children often repeat an action in play and persevere until they master it, such as making dozens of "birthday packages" to learn to tie bows, or playing on a balance beam to become a "circus performer."

Rules-based play

Kindergartners and grade-school children enjoy the challenge of making up their own rules and the social negotiation involved in adapting the rules for each play situation.

Construction play

Building houses, ships, forts, and other structures is a basic form of play that requires skill and imagination.

Make-believe play

This broad category incorporates many other play types and is rich with language, problem-solving, and imagination. It frequently begins with "Let's pretend" and goes on to include anything children might have experienced or imagined.

Symbolic play

Children take an object at hand and convert it into the toy or prop they need through a fluid process of fantasy or imagination.

Language play

Children develop mastery by playing with words, rhymes, verses, and songs they make up or change. They tell stories and dramatize them. They are fascinated by foreign languages, especially when they are presented playfully in story, verse, or song.

Playing with the arts

Children integrate all forms of art into their play, using whatever materials are at hand to draw, model, create music, perform puppet shows, and so on. They explore the arts and use them to express their feelings and ideas.

Sensory play

Most children enjoy playing with dirt, sand, mud, water, and other materials with different textures, sounds, and smells. Such play develops the senses.

Rough-and-tumble play

This fundamental form of play is found in animals as well as human children. Animals know how to play roughly without injury by rounding their body gestures and not aiming for dominance. Children can be helped to do the same if their play becomes too aggressive.

Risk-taking play

Children extend their abilities through risky play and learn to master challenging environments. They generally know how far they can go without actually hurting themselves. Regrettably, most current play spaces are designed to be as risk-free as possible, giving children little chance to assess risks and set their own boundaries.

> If problem-solving, communication, collaboration, innovation, and creative thinking are to remain part of our legacy as a species, then play must be restored to its rightful place at the heart of childhood.

Many of the capacities developed through child-initiated and child-directed play are the very ones most vital for the child's future and, indeed, for the future of our planet: problem-solving, communication, collaboration, innovation, and creative thinking. If these essential capacities are to remain part of our legacy as a species then play must be restored to its rightful place at the heart of childhood—and that includes kindergarten education. Without play in early childhood, cognitive, social, emotional, and physical development is at risk—and we are all thus endangered.

Keys to a Playful Kindergarten

Switching from a didactic approach to one with rich opportunities for play presents this risk: the tendency to go to the opposite extreme—a laissez-faire classroom where chaos reigns. Some key elements that contribute to a healthy balance in a play-based kindergarten are:

Setting the example. Purposeful adult activity inspires children's play. Parents often complain that their children like to play underfoot while they are cooking or doing other work. Typically, children want to help with adult work for a little while and then carry that inspiration into their play. They want to know what it feels like to read a book, cook a meal, chop wood, and do all the other things they see adults doing. They imitate the adults' outer gestures and inner mood. One can describe this as participatory learning, for the child participates in the adult's activity at every level. It is both physical and cognitive, with a great deal of the social and the emotional added in.

A balanced schedule. If a play period is too short, the children cannot become deeply engaged and develop complex scenarios. If it is too long, the play disintegrates. Playful five-year-olds can easily play well for 60 to 90 minutes at a time, but at the beginning of the year many will not be able to focus for such an extended period. Playtime, both indoors and out, can be lengthened as children's play skills develop.

Longer periods of child-initiated play can be balanced with shorter times when children are engaged with teacher-led activities, including storytelling, reading books, singing and movement, and project activities. Kindergartners can remain focused on the teacher for about 30 minutes if they are engaged in such activities, but in the beginning of the year one may need to start with shorter amounts of time.

A full range of hands-on activities can take place during playtime or can be offered as separate pursuits. These include art experiences and practical life activities like cooking, woodworking, and gardening. Projects can be developed that impart information in an engaging way, especially if they are inspired by the children's own play ideas.

How many play sessions should a kindergarten have in a day? A full-day, six-hour kindergarten class should probably have at least three daily play periods of an hour or longer, with at least one being outdoors. This gives children adequate time to explore and develop their ideas, interests, and capacities. As we now know (see Chapter 2), many teachers are spending three hours per day in literacy and math instruction, testing, and test preparation, making this kind of attention to play impossible.

Basic rules and boundaries. Children need to experience the presence of an actively aware teacher and to feel safely held within reasonable boundaries. Teachers and children are most comfortable when there are clear boundaries that are applied flexibly. A guiding rule can be that children should engage as fully as they can in play but try not to hurt themselves or others or to damage toys and equipment.

It is not helpful to try to create a risk-free environment. Children need to learn to cope with some risk, whether it's climbing high outdoors or building high on tabletops. Most children know how to gauge themselves to do well with varying levels of risk. Some need to be encouraged to take a risk, while others need to be held back if they have an unrealistic sense of their physical abilities.

The teacher as an active presence. The teacher in a playful kindergarten plays an active role but works in subtle ways. She is aware of the children's activities and seeks ways to build on their interests. She also assesses what they need that they are not getting through their own play and finds engaging, meaningful ways to include it in the classroom through stories, projects, and other activities.

What can teachers expect when they increase the amount of play and experiential learning? Unfortunately, many children today have grown up with little support for initiating their own original play. They will endlessly imitate what they've seen on the screen but cannot generate their

> A full-day, six-hour kindergarten class should probably have at least three daily play periods of an hour or longer, with at least one being outdoors.

own ideas for play or develop them into complex play scenarios with other children. They need the help of teachers, and the teachers need to be educated in how to offer such help. Play deficits can be remedied in both children and adults, but it takes time, attention, and the help of knowledgeable people.

What can teachers do to help generate healthy, creative play?

- Encourage parents to limit or eliminate screen time and give children's own imaginations a chance to blossom. Give parents help weaning their children from screens with suggestions on how to handle key

WHAT TEACHERS CAN DO TO GENERATE HEALTHY, CREATIVE PLAY

Limit screen time

Encourage parents to limit or eliminate screen time and give children's own imaginations a chance to blossom. Give parents help weaning their children from screens with suggestions on how to handle key times when parents depend on the screen for babysitting. Parents who have gone through this process report that it is painful for a few days or a week but then becomes much easier than they expected. A common remark from such parents: "I never knew what a wonderful child I had."

Stimulate imagination

Children need active imaginations to play well. One can feed their imaginations with stories via good books read aloud and storytelling suited to the child's age. Imagination and creativity are also inspired by puppetry and plays, nursery rhymes, poems, songs, instrumental music, painting, modeling, and other art activities.

Inspire play with real work

Do real work in the presence of children, such as baking bread, cooking, woodworking, and gardening. Many children can be brought into play by first engaging them in real work for ten or fifteen minutes. Then they are inspired to play on their own. The use of the hands in both work and play is highly stimulating to the brain, a large part of which is linked to the hands.

times when parents depend on the screen for babysitting. Parents who have gone through this process report that it is painful for a few days or a week but then becomes much easier than they expected. A common remark from such parents: "I never knew what a wonderful child I had."

- Children need active imaginations to play well. One can feed their imaginations with stories via good books read aloud and storytelling suited to the child's age. Imagination and creativity are also inspired by puppetry and plays, nursery rhymes, poems, songs, instrumental music, painting, modeling, and other art activities.

- Do real work in the presence of children, such as baking bread, cooking, woodworking, and gardening. Many children can be brought into play by first engaging them in real work for ten or fifteen minutes.

> Once a kindergarten hums with play, all forms of learning take place spontaneously and deeply.

Many questions arise in play-based kindergartens: When should a teacher intervene in a child's play? How does one handle conflict in play? How does one scaffold or build on children's play without interfering with the flow of play?

These and similar questions need to be addressed in workshops and courses and through educational materials. Fortunately, once kindergarten children become skillful players, they handle much of this on their own, but the transition period can be demanding. The results, however, are incredibly rewarding. Once a kindergarten hums with play, all forms of learning take place spontaneously and deeply.

Experienced players display a high degree of competence in play. Indeed, one might say that every child has a

genius for play and is gifted and talented in this area of life. A playful kindergarten brings out the individual genius of each child and strengthens it. As education theorist Lev Vygotsky put it, "In play a child always behaves beyond his average age, above his daily behavior. In play it is as though he were a head taller than himself."[106]

Meeting Today's Challenges in the Kindergarten

It will take time to build up a movement for play-based kindergartens. Meanwhile, many teachers want to bring play into their kindergartens but are forbidden to do so by their administrators. One teacher was told by her principal that she would be fired if she let her class play for more than ten minutes *per week*. To this teacher we can only say, be resourceful. One can achieve most reasonable learning standards through a play-based curriculum using engaging, hands-on activities. This is not the same as giving children the chance to develop open-ended play, but it is a step in the right direction. It is harder to manage this approach in heavily scripted kindergartens, but even there teachers have some time that is not scripted when experiential learning can occur.

To teachers who are deeply unhappy about the loss of play in their kindergartens, we want to say that you are not alone. Many teachers are suffering at the moment, for they are being asked to meet standards they feel are unsound and to use methods they deplore. Do what you can for now in your classroom. Find allies both inside and outside the school system. Become a play advocate or a supporter of advocates. Most important, take heart. A newfound respect for play is growing, and the time for change is at hand.

For parents who see their young children under stress and who want to make changes: let your voices be heard—in meetings with teachers and administrators, at PTA and school board meetings, in state offices where standards are set—wherever there is the slightest opening for change. Parents' voices can be very effective in bringing change to public schools. Use your insights, your imagination, your strength. Join with others and begin advocating for playful kindergartens.

CHAPTER 8

RECOMMENDATIONS FOR CREATING EFFECTIVE AND HEALTHY KINDERGARTENS

THE IMPORTANCE OF PLAY to children's healthy development and learning has been documented beyond question by research, some of which is summarized in this report. Yet play is rapidly disappearing from kindergarten and early education as a whole. We believe that the stifling of play has dire consequences—not only for children but for the future of our nation. This report is meant to bring broad public attention to the crisis in our kindergartens and to spur collective action to reverse the damage now being done.

To create effective and healthy kindergartens we call on policymakers, educators, health professionals, researchers, and parents to take action as follows:

1. **Restore child-initiated play and experiential learning with the active support of teachers to their rightful place at the heart of kindergarten education.**

- Provide time and space for play to kindergartners every school day, both indoors and during recess.

- Make room in kindergarten for all types of play that contribute to children's development, including make-believe, sensory, language, construction, large- and small-motor, and mastery play.

- Engage parents and educators in discussion of the role of play and experiential learning in healthy and effective kindergartens, so that they can advocate for play with school administrators and policymakers.

2. **Reassess kindergarten standards to ensure that they promote developmentally appropriate practices, and eliminate those that do not.**

- Replace one-size-fits-all kindergarten standards with flexible guidelines based on well-grounded knowledge of children's cognitive, social, emotional, physical, and creative development.

- Recognize the differences between the kindergarten child who is an emergent reader and the first-grade child who has become an early reader. Recognize similar differences in children's learning of math, science, and other topics. Do not expect kindergarten children to achieve academic goals best suited to first-graders.

- Change developmentally inappropriate practices that cause normal child behavior and learning patterns to be wrongly labeled as misbehavior, attention disorders, or learning disabilities.

- Eliminate the practice of kindergarten retention based on inability to meet rigid standards or to pass a particular test.

3. **End the inappropriate use in kindergarten of standardized tests, which are prone to serious error especially when given to children under age eight.**

- Use alternatives to standardized assessments in kindergarten, such as teacher observations and assessment of children's work. Educate teachers in the use of these alternatives and in the risks and limitations of standardized testing of young children.

- Do not make important decisions about young children, their teachers, or their schools based solely or primarily on standardized test scores.

4. **Expand the early childhood research agenda to examine the long-term impact of current preschool and kindergarten practices on the development of children from diverse backgrounds.**

- Evaluate current kindergarten practices with qualitative as well as quantitative methods. Such research should assess children's overall health and their cognitive, social, emotional, and physical development at least until fourth grade.

- Replicate on a much larger scale the quantitative studies of kindergarten use of time and materials described in Chapter 2 of this report so that a representative sample of teachers in many different areas contribute to the full picture of current kindergarten practices.

- Investigate the associations between developmentally inappropriate kindergarten practices and behavioral and psychiatric disturbances and other health problems among young children.

5. **Give teachers of young children first-rate preparation that emphasizes the full development of the child and the importance of play, nurtures children's innate love of learning, and supports teachers' own capacities for creativity, autonomy, and integrity.**

- Make course work in child development and the use of play in the classroom mandatory in early childhood education programs.

- Give teachers professional development, mentoring, and other support in learning how to encourage and support play, especially with children who have had limited opportunity to engage in creative play or who have poor self-regulation skills.

- Help teachers communicate with parents about the importance of play and ways to support it at home and in the community.

6. **Use the crisis of play's disappearance from kindergarten to rally organizations and individuals to create a national movement for play in schools and communities.**

- Work across traditional boundaries of profession, geography, and interest group to advocate for play in classrooms, after-school and camp programs, parks and playgrounds, neighborhoods and cities.

- Establish local, state, and national play policies that recognize the importance of play for children of all ages—including the ways that play enhances physical, social, emotional, and cognitive development.

- Address the obstacles to play, such as unsafe neighborhoods, overscheduling of children's lives, excessive screen time, toys linked to entertainment media, and education that emphasizes skills, drills, and homework and undermines creativity, imagination, and overall well-being.

For further background on these recommendations, see the Alliance for Childhood's Call to Action on the Education of Young Children, which was signed by hundreds of educators and health professionals, including many leaders in these fields. Appendix A contains the full text of the Call to Action and a partial list of signers.

VIVIAN GUSSIN PALEY

AFTERWORD

YOUNG CHILDREN do not ask of each other: Where do you come from? Instead, they ask: What role will you play? Who will you and I pretend to be in a story we make up together?

From the earliest age, children begin to practice their imaginary characters, their separate visions of pleasure and pain, of strength and weakness, of love and loss. By the time they enter kindergarten they are ready to build complex worlds in which friendship and fairness are inalienable rights, and every child has a secure place in an intimate community.

A kindergarten without a substantial playtime puts everyone at a disadvantage, for play is still the primary reality for its members. Play contains the only set of circumstances children understand from beginning to end. "I can do this well," the kindergartners seem to say. "I can be this effectively. I understand what is happening to me and to the other children."

Within this familiar process of inventing new characters and plots, of pretending to be someone else in another place, the children continue to develop the intuitive and universal language that binds us all together. In a kindergarten where children play, the teacher has an opportunity to study each child's individual style and story, and to introduce all manner of new material into a functioning social community. In a kindergarten where children play, children learn to focus their imaginations in ever more complex ways and, in the enlivened environment, are ready to conquer new problems.

Let us open our kindergartens again to the world's most natural learning tool: play.

A CALL TO ACTION ON THE EDUCATION OF YOUNG CHILDREN

WE ARE DEEPLY CONCERNED that current trends in early education, fueled by political pressure, are leading to an emphasis on unproven methods of academic instruction and unreliable standardized testing that can undermine learning and damage young children's healthy development.

Many states are moving toward universal preschool so that all children can benefit from early education. We strongly support these efforts, provided that preschool programs are based on well-established knowledge of how children learn and how to lay a foundation for lifelong learning—not on educational fads. *We call for early education that emphasizes experiential, hands-on activities, open-ended creative play, and caring human relationships.*

Preschool education must not follow the same path that has led kindergartens toward intense academic instruction with little or no time for child-initiated learning. If such practices were effective for five-year-olds, we would have seen better long-term results by now. *We call for a reversal of the pushing down of the curriculum that has transformed kindergarten into de facto first grade.*

Education is not a race where the prize goes to the one who finishes first. To help young children develop literacy and a lifelong love of learning we need to respect and, when needed, to strengthen their individual abilities and drive to learn. Instead, current trends in early education policy and practice heighten pressure and stress in children's lives, which can contribute to behavioral and learning problems. *We call for research on the causes of increased levels of anger, misbehavior, and school expulsion among young children.*

Justified concern for low-income children, who often lag academically, has been a powerful force behind the current overemphasis on early instruction in literacy and math. This well-intentioned but misguided policy may actually put children at increased risk of school failure by denying them positive early learning experiences. *We call for additional research that examines the long-term impact of different preschool and kindergarten practices on children from diverse backgrounds.*

Creative play that children can control is central to their physical, emotional, and cognitive growth. It contributes greatly to their language development, social skills, and problem-solving capacities, and lays an essential foundation for later academic learning. Yet many children do not have the opportunity to develop their capacity for socio-dramatic play. Preschool is the place to intervene and restore childhood play. *We call for teacher education that emphasizes the full development of the child including the importance of play, nurtures children's innate love of learning, and supports teachers' own capacities for creativity, autonomy, and integrity.*

This statement, drafted by the Alliance for Childhood, has been endorsed by hundreds of concerned citizens including those listed on the following page. Organizations are included for identification purposes only.

Enola G. Aird, Founder and Director, The Motherhood Project, Institute for American Values, New York City

Robert Anderson, California Department of Education (retired), Fair Oaks, CA

Lyda Beardsley, Ph.D., Executive Director, Trio Foundation, Berkeley, CA

Barbara Beatty, Associate Professor and Chair, Department of Education, Wellesley College, Wellesley, MA

Marilyn B. Benoit, M.D., past president, American Academy of Child and Adolescent Psychiatry, Washington, DC

T. Berry Brazelton, M.D., Professor of Pediatrics Emeritus, Harvard Medical School, Boston

Michael Brody, M.D., child psychiatrist, University of Maryland, Potomac, MD

Stuart L. Brown, M.D., psychiatrist and founder, The National Institute for Play, Carmel Valley, CA

Nancy Carlsson-Paige, Professor, Lesley University, Cambridge, MA

Virginia Casper, Associate Dean, Bank Street College of Education, New York City

Sherry M. Cleary, Executive Director, NYC Early Childhood Professional Development Institute, City University of New York

Renatta M. Cooper, Commissioner, First 5 Los Angeles

William Crain, Professor of Psychology, City College of New York

Linda Darling-Hammond, Charles Ducommun Professor of Education, Stanford University, Stanford, CA

Libby Doggett, Deputy Director, Pew Center on the States, Washington, DC

Eleanor Duckworth, Professor of Education, Harvard University, Cambridge, MA

Elliot Eisner, Lee Jacks Professor of Education, Stanford University, Stanford, CA

David Elkind, Professor Emeritus of Child Development, Tufts University, Medford, MA

Margery Franklin, Ph.D., Director Emerita, Child Development Institute, Sarah Lawrence College, Bronxville, NY

Howard Gardner, Hobbs Professor of Cognition and Education, Harvard University, Cambridge, MA

Daniel Goleman, co-founder, Collaborative for Academic, Social and Emotional Learning, University of Illinois, Chicago

Dr. Jane Goodall, DBE, Founder, Jane Goodall Institute and U.N. Messenger of Peace, Arlington, VA

John I. Goodlad, University of Washington and Institute for Educational Inquiry, Seattle

Stanley Greenspan, M.D., Clinical Professor of Psychiatry and Pediatrics, George Washington University Medical Center, Bethesda, MD

Jane M. Healy, Ph.D., educational psychologist, author, and lecturer, Vail, CO

Olga Jarrett, Associate Professor of Early Childhood Education, Georgia State University, Atlanta

Lilian G. Katz, Professor Emerita, University of Illinois, Urbana-Champaign

Tovah Klein, Ph.D., Director, Barnard College Center for Toddler Development, New York City

Edgar Klugman, Professor Emeritus, Wheelock College, Boston

Jonathan Kozol, author of *Shame of the Nation*, Byfield, MA

Velma LaPoint, Ph.D., Professor of Child Development, School of Education, Howard University, Washington, DC

Diane Levin, Professor of Education, Wheelock College, Boston

Susan Linn, Ed.D., Instructor in Psychiatry, Harvard Medical School, Boston

Yeou-Cheng Ma, M.D., developmental pediatrician, Albert Einstein College of Medicine, New York City

Kathleen McCartney, Dean, Harvard Graduate School of Education, Cambridge, MA

Deborah Meier, Senior Scholar, New York University, New York City

Samuel J. Meisels, President, Erikson Institute, Chicago

Thomas Moore, author, *Care of the Soul*, Amherst, NH

Pedro Noguera, Professor of Teaching and Learning and Director, Metropolitan Center for Urban Education, New York University

Vivian Gussin Paley, teacher and writer, Chicago

Bruce D. Perry, M.D., Senior Fellow, Child Trauma Academy, Houston, TX

Jane P. Perry, Ph.D., Teacher and Research Coordinator, Harold E. Jones Child Study Center, University of California, Berkeley

Alvin Poussaint, M.D., Professor of Psychiatry, Harvard Medical School and Judge Baker Children's Center, Boston

Kyle Pruett, M.D., Clinical Professor of Child Psychiatry, Yale University School of Medicine, New Haven, CT

Alvin Rosenfeld, M.D., child and adolescent psychiatrist, co-author, *The Over-Scheduled Child*, New York City

Larry Schweinhart, President, High/Scope Educational Research Foundation, Ypsilanti, MI

Dorothy G. Singer, Senior Research Scientist, Child Study Center, Yale University, New Haven, CT

Jerome L. Singer, Professor Emeritus of Psychology, Yale University, New Haven, CT

Deborah Stipek, Dean, Stanford University School of Education, Stanford, CA

Rosario Villasana-Ruiz, Professor, City College of San Francisco

Frank Wilson, M.D., Clinical Professor of Neurology (retired), Stanford University School of Medicine, Stanford, CA

George Wood, Director, The Forum for Education and Democracy, Amesville, OH

Definitions

Play: The word *play* is commonly used by early childhood educators and researchers to include activities designed by adults and often led by adults (like computer games, organized sports, and even games designed to teach literacy or math skills) as well as those initiated and led by children (playing tag, acting out make-believe stories, building with blocks, pretending to be horses romping in a pasture). In this report we use *play* only to refer to those activities that are freely chosen and directed by children and arise from intrinsic motivation. This is the kind of play that is most critical for children's overall development—and is most endangered by current early childhood policies. It emerges from the child's own drive to make sense of the world and is not imposed, directed, or controlled by adult agendas. Sometimes, however, adults need to intervene to help children get started on play or to redirect them from destructive play. The wise adult steps back as soon as she senses that the children can carry the play on their own.

Playful learning: Many teachers recognize that play and hands-on experiences are the most powerful modes of learning for young children. Therefore, when they want children to learn some specific material, either because they see a need for the child to know it or because standards dictate that it must be taught, they try to make their lessons as playful and experiential as possible. While *playful learning* is an important part of kindergarten education, it should not be confused with child-initiated play. *Focused learning through play* and *experiential learning* are also ways to describe classroom practices linked to adult goals.

Choice time: Few schools actually use the word *play* in describing their kindergarten programs and curricula, even though, when asked, most teachers and many administrators will agree that play is important for young children. But the term itself has become controversial, a code word that represents in many quarters a feel-good, undisciplined, lazy approach to schooling. Thus most kindergartens now refer euphemistically to *choice time*, and sometimes to *center time*, to indicate periods during the school day when children can choose their activities. In the past children were often allowed to play rather freely in centers, such as the housekeeping center or nature center, but direct observation of kindergarten classrooms today shows that real play (as defined above) often does not take place, even in choice time or center time. Today's kindergartens often have curriculum goals for each center, so choice time means choosing which area of the curriculum the child will work on. The child then performs predetermined actions within the centers rather than freely choosing how to interact with the materials in the center.

Center time: See "Choice time."

Developmentally appropriate: The term *developmentally appropriate* is generally used to refer to educational and child care practices that are based on a developmental view of the child—an understanding of the stages of physical, cognitive, emotional, and social development that children move through as they progress from infancy through toddlerhood, preschool, kindergarten, and the early elementary grades. This view rejects the idea that children are miniature adults, as well as the assumption that the earlier a child learns to do something—such as reading, doing arithmetic, or using a computer—the more successful the child will be in school and adult life. Developmentally appropriate activities and practices are chosen because they accord with or enhance the general patterns and stages of child development and suit the needs of the individual child.

Direct instruction: This term was used in some important research studies (such as the High/Scope Preschool Curriculum Comparison Study) to describe a highly scripted approach to early education, in which the activities and the teacher's words and interventions were carefully circumscribed and the children were given little or no choice in how they spent their time. In recent years, *direct instruction* has been used in a significantly different sense, to describe, for example, the intentional teaching of phonics skills or mathematical processes as a discrete activity. Because of this confusion, we will in general avoid using the term in this report but will refer to *teacher-directed* or *didactic instruction,* or to *scripted teaching.* (See below.)

Child-initiated: *Child-initiated* activities are motivated by the intrinsic interests and needs of the child. This quality is essential for play, in the sense that we use the word in this document (see above). Research evidence indicates that child-initiated, rather than teacher-directed, learning leads to the most profound and long-lasting positive effects on the child.

Teacher-directed: During *teacher-directed* activities the teacher is imparting content to a group of children. All eyes are on the teacher or on the activities she has initiated. The content may be a book that is being read, a story being told, a puppet play being performed, or verses and poems being shared. But it may also be a curriculum script being read, or literacy and math lessons. Every classroom has some time devoted to teacher-directed activities, but when allowed to make their own choices teachers vary as to how much time is spent in this form of teaching and what the content is. The more prescriptive the curriculum, the less choice the teacher has.

Didactic instruction: *Didactic instruction* in kindergarten emphasizes the children's acquisition of discrete facts and skills, usually in an atmosphere of serious, purposeful study. It requires children to sit still and pay attention to the teacher and the work at hand. This kind of teaching was considered inappropriate and ineffective in kindergarten until recent years. Now it is increasingly common, although there is little research showing long-term gains from this approach.

Scripted teaching: In *scripted teaching* programs, the teacher follows a regimented and invariable routine—literally a script—in which prescribed activities and words are used and others are prohibited. These curricula are linked to standardized tests given at frequent intervals to measure children's progress in learning the designated facts and skills. Interest in scripted teaching ballooned during the administration of President George W. Bush. Its use was encouraged by the Department of Education's Reading First program, and it can be found in many urban schools. (See Chapter 5 for more details.)

Standards: *Standards* are goals for academic achievement and exist for a wide range of subjects. Initially, the fact that standards would apply to all children was seen as a step toward equality in education. Now, critics argue that once standards are in place the curriculum is necessarily narrowed down. Thus, rather than lifting the work force to a higher level of learning, which was one of the original reasons for setting standards, they may be holding many children back. When standards were first called for, they focused on high school. Now there are standards for everyone, including kindergartners and preschoolers. Efforts to meet early childhood standards have severely limited the kinds of activities offered to children. (See Chapter 3 for more details.)

ENDNOTES

Chapter 1: Introduction

[1] Written comment from one of the kindergarten teachers in the Fuligni and Hong study described in Chapter 2. Participants in the study were assured that their identities would remain confidential.

[2] "High-Stakes Testing: A Statement of Concern and Call to Action," position statement of the Alliance for Childhood (2001); http://www.allianceforchildhood.net/news/histakes_test_position_statement.htm.

[3] "Children from Birth to Five: Academics Versus Play," policy statement of the Alliance for Childhood (2003); http://www.allianceforchildhood.net/news/articles.htm.

[4] "Call to Action on the Education of Young Children," position statement of the Alliance for Childhood (2005). See Appendix A.

[5] See note #1 above.

[6] See http://americanjournalofplay.press.uiuc.edu/1/3/singer.html.

[7] See http://ies.ed.gov/ncee/wwc/reports/beginning_reading/open_court/index.asp.

[8] See http://ies.ed.gov/ncee/pdf/20094039.pdf.

[9] See http://aappolicy.aappublications.org/cgi/content/full/pediatrics;119/1/182.

[10] See http://www.highscope.org/Content.asp?ContentId=257.

[11] "Preschool Comparison," High/Scope Research Foundation; http://www.highscope.org/Content.asp?ContentId=241.

[12] "Reading First Program Draws Fresh Criticism in GAO Report," *Chronicle of Higher Education*, March 23, 2007; http://chronicle.com/news/article/1860/reading-first-program-draws-fresh-criticism-in-gao-report.

[13] L. B. Wiedey and J. M. Lichtenstein, "Academic Stress in Kindergarten Children," ERIC document ED310865 (1987).

[14] Matt Burgard, "Into School, Out of Control," *Hartford Courant*, April 2, 2007; http://www.hartfordinfo.org/issues/documents/Education/htfd_courant_040207.asp.

[15] Elena Bodrova and Deborah J. Leong, "Uniquely Preschool," *Educational Leadership*, September 2005, pp. 46-47; http://www.mscd.edu/extendedcampus/toolsofthemind/assets/pdf/Educational_leadership_sep05.pdf.

Chapter 3: Reassessing Standards

[16] *A Nation at Risk* (1983) http://www.ed.gov/pubs/NatAtRisk/risk.html, p.1.

[17] Vivian Gussin Paley, *A Child's Work: The Importance of Fantasy Play*, Chicago: University of Chicago Press (2004), p. 45.

[18] "Literacy Guide: Early Literacy Development," Bank Street College of Education; http://www.bnkst.edu/literacyguide/early.html.

[19] "Preschool Comparison," High/Scope Educational Research Foundation; http://www.highscope.org/Content.asp?ContentId=241.

[20] Rebecca A. Marcon, "Moving Up the Grades: Relationship Between Preschool Model and Later School Success," *Early Childhood Research and Practice*, Vol. 4, No. 1 (Spring 2002); http://ecrp.uiuc.edu/v4n1/marcon.html.

[21] Developing Early Literacy: Report of the National Early Literacy Panel, National Institute for Literacy (January 8, 2009); http://www.nifl.gov/nifl/publications/pdf/NELPSummary.pdf.

[22] David Dickinson, Kathy Hirsh-Pasek, Susan Neuman, Roberta M. Golinkoff, and Margaret Buchinal, "The Language of Emergent Literacy: A Response to the National Institute for Literacy Report on Early Literacy," obtained through private communication. See note 66 for further information.

[23] Kathleen Kennedy Manzo, "Experts Eschew Narrow Reading of Early-Literacy Study," *Education Week* (January 8, 2009; updated January 21, 2009); http://www.edweek.org/login.html?source=http://www.edweek.org/ew/articles/2009/01/08/18read.h28.html&destination=http://www.edweek.org/ew/articles/2009/01/08/18read.h28.html&levelId=1000.

[24] Ibid.

[25] *Developing Early Literacy: Report of the National Early Literacy Panel*, National Institute for Literacy (January 8, 2009); http://www.nifl.gov/nifl/publications/pdf/NELPSummary.pdf, p. 218.

[26] *English–Language Arts Content Standards for California Public Schools: Kindergarten Through Grade Twelve*, kindergarten standard for reading 1.6, p. 9; http://www.cde.ca.gov/be/st/ss/documents/elacontentstnds.pdf.

[27] *English–Language Arts Content Standards for California Public Schools: Kindergarten Through Grade Twelve*, kindergarten standard for writing 1.4, p. 11; http://www.cde.ca.gov/be/st/ss/documents/elacontentstnds.pdf.

[28] Tennessee Kindergarten Reading Standard K.1.06 (c); http://www.tennessee.gov/education/ci/english/reading_k.shtml.

[29] "A Broader, Bolder Approach to Education," p.2; http://www.boldapproach.org/bold_approach_full_statement.pdf.

[30] Shane R. Jimerson, Phillip Ferguson, Angela D. Whipple, Gabrielle E. Anderson, and Michael J. Dalton, "Exploring the Association Between Grade Retention and Dropout: A Longitudinal Study Examining Socio-Emotional, Behavioral, and Achievement Characteristics of Retained Students," *The California School Psychologist*, Vol. 7 (2002); http://education.ucsb.edu/jimerson/retention/CSP_RetentionDropout2002.pdf, p. 14.

[31] "Grade-Level Retention in Public Schools," Texas Education Agency (2005); http://ritter.tea.state.tx.us/research/pdfs/retention_2003-04.pdf, p. 14.

[32] Kindergarten Readiness Issues Group, "North Carolina Early Grade Retention in the Age of Accountability," Partners in Research Forum; Chapel Hill: The University of North Carolina, FPG Child Development Institute (2003). www.fpg.unc.edu/~pir/retention_brief.pdf, p.2.

[33] Anita B. Sakowicz, "The Effect of Retention, in Grade One, on the Slow Reader," M.A. Project, Kean College of New Jersey, April 1996. Cited in Anne S. Robertson, "When Retention Is Recommended, What Should Parents Do?" ERIC Digest, May 1997, ED 408 102; http://www.ericdigests.org/1998-1/parents.htm.

[34] Kindergarten Readiness Issues Group, op. cit., p.3.

[35] National Association of School Psychologists, (n.d.). "Should My Child Repeat a Grade?," Bethesda, MD: NASP. Cited in Anne S. Robertson, "When Retention Is Recommended, What Should Parents Do?" ERIC Digest, May 1997, ED 408 102; http://www.ericdigests.org/1998-1/parents.htm.

[36] Jill Setencich, "The Impact of Early Grade Retention on the Academic Achievement and Self-Esteem of Seventh and Eighth Grade Students," p. 7. Paper presented at the Annual Convention of the National Association of School Psychologists, Seattle, WA, March 1994. Cited in Anne S. Robertson, "When Retention Is Recommended, What Should Parents Do?" ERIC Digest, May 1997, ED 408 102; http://www.ericdigests.org/1998-1/parents.htm.

[37] "Still Unacceptable Trends in Kindergarten Entry and Placement," position statement endorsed by the National Association for the Education of Young Children, March 2001; http://www.naeyc.org/about/positions/pdf/psunacc.pdf.

[38] Samuel J. Meisels and Fong-Ruey Liaw, "Failure in Grade: Do Retained Students Catch Up?" *Journal of Educational Research*, 87 (2) (1993), pp. 69-77. EJ 476 840; http://www.ericdigests.org/1998-1/parents.htm.

[39] Yingying Dong, "Kept Back to Get Ahead? Kindergarten Retention and Academic Performance," Department of Economics, Boston College (May 2008); p. 28; http://www2.bc.edu/~dongyi/Research/K_Retention_YDong.pdf.

[40] "Study: Income Levels Affect Kids' IQ, Behavior," *School Library Journal* (May 31, 2007); http://www.schoollibraryjournal.com/article/CA6447836.html.

Chapter 4: Out-of-Control Testing

[41] See, for example, "20/20 Concept Explained," Steve MacDonald & Associates (Profit Improvement Specialists); http://www.stevemacdonald.com/20-20-system/20-20-system-concept-explained.htm; also Thomas Lindsay Jackson and Karen R. Jones, *Implementing a Lean Management System*, Productivity Press (1996).

[42] Elissa Gootman, "Schools Raise Bar for Classes for the Gifted," *New York Times* (October 30, 2007).

[43] Elissa Gootman, "A Plan to Test the City's Youngest Pupils," *New York Times* (August 26, 2008).

[44] Ibid.

[45] Stephen Metcalf, "Reading Between the Lines," *The Nation* (January 11, 2002).

[46] "Mayor Michael R. Bloomberg Testifies on Urban Education Reform Before the U.S. House Committee on Education and Labor," on New York City's web site. See http://www.nyc.gov/portal/site/nycgov/menuitem.c0935b9a57bb4ef3daf2f1c701c789a0/index.jsp?pageID=mayor_press_release&catID=1194&doc_name=http%3A%2F%2Fwww.nyc.gov%2Fhtml%2Fom%2Fhtml%2F2008b%2Fpr279-08.html&cc=unused1978&rc=1194&ndi=1.

[47] Jennifer Jennings and Sherman Dorn, "The Proficiency Trap: New York City's Achievement Gap Revisited," *Teachers College Record* (Sept. 8, 2008); http://www.tcrecord.org/Content.asp?ContentID=15366.

[48] Ibid.

[49] "Still Unacceptable Trends in Kindergarten Entry and Placement," position statement of the NAEYC (2000 Revision), http://www.naeyc.org/about/positions/Psunacc.asp.

[50] Ibid.

[51] "About UKTLV," United Kindergarten Teachers of Las Vegas web site: http://uktlv.org/about.html.

[52] National Association of School Psychologists, "Position Statement on Early Childhood Assessment," http://www.nasponline.org/about_nasp/pospaper_eca.aspx.

[53] Vito Perrone, "ACEI Position Paper on Standardized Testing," Association for Childhood Education International, 1991; http://www.acei.org/onstandard.htm.

[54] Ibid.

[55] Jay P. Heubert and Robert M. Hauser, editors; Committee on Appropriate Test Use, National Research Council, *High Stakes: Testing for Tracking, Promotion, and Graduation*, National Academies Press (1999), p. 279; http://www.nap.edu/openbook.php?record_id=6336&page=279.

[56] Ibid.

[57] Catherine E. Snow and Susan B. Van Hemel, editors, National Research Council of the National Academies, *Early Childhood Assessment: Why, What, and How*, National Academies Press (2008), p. 10; http://books.nap.edu/openbook.php?isbn=0309124654&page=10.

[58] "Evaluating Children in Preschools and Early Childhood Programs," *e!Science News* (August 4, 2008); http://esciencenews.com/articles/2008/08/04/evaluating.children.preschools.and.early.childhood.programs.

[59] Ibid.

[60] Ibid.

[61] Ibid.

Chapter 5: The Scripted Kindergarten

[62] Sarah Colt, "Do Scripted Lessons Work—Or Not?" *Making Schools Work*, Public Broadcasting Service web site (2005); http://www.pbs.org/makingschoolswork/sbs/sfa/lessons.html.

[63] L. J. Schweinhart and D. P. Weikart, "Seeing the Tree as Part of the Forest: A Response to Engelmann's Critique of the High/Scope Preschool Curriculum Study." Unpublished. Available from High/Scope Educational Research Foundation: www.highscope.org.

[64] Anita Ede, "Scripted Curriculum: Is It a Prescription for Success?" *Childhood Education* (Fall 2006); http://findarticles.com/p/articles/mi_qa3614/is_200610/ai_n17189994.

[65] The U.C.L.A. study of Los Angeles kindergartens, reported in Chapter 2, for example, found that 88 percent of the teachers surveyed were using Open Court Reading, one of the most popular of the current scripted literacy curricula. See page 27 of this report.

[66] Henry Morgan, *The Imagination of Early Childhood Education*, Westport, CT: Bergin & Garvey (1999); pg. 163.

[67] High/Scope Educational Research Foundation, "Preschool Comparison"; http://www.highscope.org/Content.asp?ContentId=241.

[68] Promising Practices Network evaluation of Direct Instruction; http://www.promisingpractices.net/program.asp?programid=146.

[69] Robert E. Land and Margaret Moustafa, "Are Scripted Reading Instruction Programs a Benefit or a Bane?: A research response," (2002) pg. 1; http://instructional1.calstatela.edu/mmousta/Scripted_Reading_Instruction.pdf.

[70] Margaret Moustafa and Robert Land, "The Research Base of Open Court and Its Translation into Instructional Policy in California"; http://instructional1.calstatela.edu/mmousta/The_Research_Base_of_Open_Court_and_Its_Translation_into_Instructional_Policy_in_California.htm. For a more detailed presentation of the Land and Moustafa research see "Scripted Reading Response: Help or Hindrance?" in *Reading for Profit: How the Bottom Line Leaves Kids Behind*, Bess Altwerger, editor; Portsmouth: Heinemann (2005); pp. 63-77.

[71] U.S. Department of Education evaluation of Open Court Reading program (2008); http://ies.ed.gov/ncee/wwc/reports/beginning_reading/open_court/index.asp.

[72] U.S. Department of Education, "Reading First Impact Study, Final Report" (2008), Executive Summary, p.v; http://ies.ed.gov/ncee/pdf/20094039.pdf.

[73] Kathleen Kennedy Manzo, "No Effect on Comprehension Seen From 'Reading First'," *Education Week* (November 19, 2008); http://www.edweek.org/login.html?source=http://www.edweek.org/ew/articles/2008/11/18/14read.h28.html&destination=http://www.edweek.org/ew/articles/2008/11/18/14read.h28.html&levelId=2100.

[74] Press release from U.S. House Education and Labor Committee (April 20, 2007); http://www.house.gov/apps/list/speech/edlabor_dem/rel042007rf.html.

Chapter 6: Play and Children's Health

[75] From a talk by Gillian McNamee, Ph.D., co-sponsored by the Alliance for Childhood and Franklin Park (IL) Parks Department. Franklin Park, IL, May 11, 2006. McNamee is director of teacher education at the Erikson Institute in Chicago; she spoke of four vital signs of health in children: eating, sleeping, toileting, and play. See http://www.allianceforchildhood.net/pdf_files/playwork_Chicago_2006.pdf.

[76] Kenneth R. Ginsburg, M.D., M.S.Ed., and the Committee on Communications and the Committee on Psychosocial Aspects of Child and Family Health, "The Importance of Play in Promoting Healthy Child Development and Maintaining Strong Parent-Child Bonds," *Pediatrics*, Vol. 119, No. 1 (January 2007), pp. 182–191 (doi:10.1542/peds.2006–2697). For press release and link to report see http://aappolicy.aappublications.org/cgi/content/full/pediatrics;119/1/182.

[77] For further information on playwork see the Alliance for Childhood fact sheet "Playwork and Play" at http://www.allianceforchildhood.net/projects/play/pdf_files/Playwork.pdf.

[78] Ben Fenton, "Junk Culture 'Is Poisoning Our Children'," London *Telegraph* (Sept. 13, 2006); http://www.telegraph.co.uk/news/1528642/Junk-culture-'is-poisoning-our-children'.html; for the full text of letter, see http://www.suepalmer.co.uk/articles/Letter.pdf.

[79] Based on statistics from "Generation M: Media in the Lives of 8–18-Year-Olds," Henry J. Kaiser Family Foundation (March 2005). Total figures reported are 6+ hours per day of media, which includes about ¾ hour for reading. Most media are used indoors. http://www.kff.org/entmedia/upload/Executive-Summary-Generation-M-Media-in-the-Lives-of-8-18-Year-olds.pdf.

[80] Sandra Hofferth, "American Children's Outdoor and Indoor Leisure Time," in Elizabeth Goodenough, editor, *A Place for Play*, Carmel Valley, CA: National Institute for Play (2008), p.42.

[81] "Calories burned in 30 minutes for people of three different weights," *Harvard Heart Letter* (July 2004), https://www.health.harvard.edu/newsweek/Calories-burned-in-30-minutes-of-leisure-and-routine-activities.htm.

[82] Pam Belluck, "Children's Life Expectancy Being Cut Short by Obesity," *New York Times* (March 17, 2005); http://www.nytimes.com/2005/03/17/health/17obese.html.

[83] Sharna Olfman, editor, *No Child Left Different*, Westport, CT: Praeger (2006), p. 1.

[84] "Recognizing Children's Successes in All Areas May Prevent Teenage Depression," University of Missouri News Bureau (January 8, 2009); http://munews.missouri.edu/news-releases/2009/0108-herman-children.php.

[85] Bob Herbert, "6-Year-Olds Under Arrest," *New York Times* op-ed page (April 9, 2007); http://select.nytimes.com/2007/04/09/opinion/09herbert.html?_r=1.

[86] Matt Burgard, "Into School, Out of Control: Nowadays, Even the Youngest Students Turn to Violence," *Hartford Courant* (April 2, 2007).

[87] Sara Bennett and Nancy Kalish, *The Case Against Homework*, New York: Three Rivers Press (2006), p. 109.

[88] Burgard, op. cit.

[89] Mayor's Commission for Children, "Aggression in the Kindergarten," Springfield, MO (August 2005); http://www.ci.springfield.mo.us/children_commission/pdf/white_paper8505.pdf.

[90] Claudia Wallis, "Does Kindergarten Need Cops?" Time Magazine (December 7, 2003); http://www.time.com/time/magazine/article/0,9171,1101031215-556865,00.html?cnn=yes.

[91] Ibid.

[92] Walter S. Gilliam, "Pre–K Students Expelled at More Than Three Times the Rate of K–12 Students," New Haven, CT: Yale University Office of Public Affairs (May 17, 2005); http://opa.yale.edu/news/article.aspx?id=4271.

[93] Liana Heitin, "Boy Problems" (interview with journalist Peg Tyre), *Teacher Magazine* (Sept. 30, 2008); http://www.teachermagazine.org/tm/articles/2008/09/30/08boyproblems.h19.html?r=1209400783.

[94] "Pre-Kindergarten Expulsion in Texas Reaches Alarming Rates," *EdNews* (May 11, 2008); http://ednews.org/articles/25486/1/Pre-Kindergarten-Expulsion-in-Texas-Reaches-Alarming-Rates/Page1.html.

[95] "Preschool Comparison," High/Scope Educational Research Foundation; http://www.highscope.org/Content.asp?ContentId=241.

[96] Kathy Hirsh-Pasek, Roberta Michnick Golinkoff, Laura E. Berk, and Dorothy Singer, *A Mandate for Playful Learning in Preschool: Compiling the Scientific Evidence*, Oxford University Press (2009).

[97] Alliance for Childhood, "A Call to Action on the Education of Young Children," http://www.allianceforchildhood.net/pdf_files/Call_to_Action_on_Young_Children.pdf.

[98] L. A. Barnett and B. Storm, "Play, Pleasure, and Pain: The Reduction of Anxiety Through Play," *Leisure Sciences*, 4 (1981), pp. 161–175; cited in Laura E. Berk, Tricia D. Mann, and Amy T. Ogan, "Make-Believe Play: Wellspring for Development of Self-Regulation," Illinois State University, http://udel.edu/~roberta/play/BerkMannOgan.pdf. See also a similar study reported by Melinda Wenner in "The Serious Need for Play," *Scientific American Mind* (February/March 2009), p. 27.

Chapter 7: The Playful Kindergarten

[99] Melinda Wenner, "The Serious Need for Play," *Scientific American Mind* (February-March 2009); http://www.sciam.com/article.cfm?id=the-serious-need-for-play&page=5.

[100] Vivian Gussin Paley, *A Child's Work: The Importance of Fantasy Play*, Chicago: University of Chicago Press (2004), p. 33.

[101] Ibid., p. 46.

[102] Based on the research of Smilansky and Shefatya, *Facilitating Play: A Medium for Promoting Cognitive, Socio-emotional, and Academic Development in Young Children*, Gaithersburg, MD: Psychological and Educational Publications (1990). Cited in Bodrova and Leong, "The Importance of Being Playful," *Educational Leadership*, Vol. 60, No. 7 (April 2003), pp. 50–53; http://pdonline.ascd.org/pd_online/substitute/el200304_bodrova.html.

[103] Based on the research of K. Roskos and J. F. Christie (editors), *Play and Literacy in Early Childhood: Research from Multiple Perspectives*, Mahwah, NJ: Erlbaum (2000). Cited in Bodrova and Leong, "The Importance of Being Playful," *Educational Leadership*, Vol. 60, No. 7 (April 2003), pp. 50–53; http://pdonline.ascd.org/pd_online/substitute/el200304_bodrova.html.

[104] Kathy Hirsh-Pasek et al., op. cit., p. 54.

[105] Bonnie Neugebauer, "The Spirit of Adult Play," Child Care Information Exchange, http://ccie.com/catalog/product_info.php?products_id=5008926&search=&category.

[106] Lev Vygotsky, *Mind in Society: The Development of Higher Psychological Processes*, Cambridge, MA: Harvard University Press (1978), p.102.